DENG XIAOPING

A LERNER BIOGRAPHY

Leader in a Changing China

WHITNEY STEWART

Lerner Publications Company /Minneapolis

To all those who suffered trying to build a stronger China

Lerner Publications Company
A division of Lerner Publishing Group
241 First Avenue North
Minneapolis, MN 55401 U.S.A.

Website address: www.lernerbooks.com

Library of Congress Cataloging-in-Publication Data

Stewart, Whitney, 1959–
    Deng Xiaoping / by Whitney Stewart.
        p.   cm. — (A Lerner biography)
    Includes bibliographical references and index.
        Summary: Traces the life and career of the Chinese Communist leader
    who brought reforms and international trade to China in the 1980s.
        ISBN 0-8225-4962-X (lib. bdg. : alk. paper)
        1. Teng Hsiao-p'ing, 1904–1997—Juvenile literature. 2. Heads of state—
    China—Biography—Juvenile literature. [1. Teng Hsiao-p'ing, 1904–1997
    2. Heads of state.] I. Title. II. Series.
    DS778.T39 S8   2001
    951.05'092—dc21   00-008330

Manufactured in the United States of America
1 2 3 4 5 6 – JR – 06 05 04 03 02 01

Contents

Emperors and empresses of the Qing dynasty lived in the
Forbidden City in Beijing, a compound of many beautiful, stately
buildings.

INTRODUCTION

Deng Xiaoping lived in China during a period that was marked by imperial rule, revolutionary republican organizations, warlord battles, foreign invasions, Communist revolution, and prodemocracy demonstrations. Deng was involved with many of those historic twentieth-century events. But, his was just one lifetime in China's history, which extends over more than five thousand years. To understand Deng's life, it is important to understand China's political history. Why? Because Deng was a political man. Chinese politics shaped him, and he helped shape them.

In 1644, China's Ming dynasty (family of rulers) was overthrown by Manchu invaders. The Manchus were a non-Chinese people who lived in the hilly, forested regions and the plains northeast of China. After the Manchus took over, China's land was divided among Manchu noblemen, imperial clansmen, and the four Manchu military groups, which were distinguished by their colored banners. The Chinese people had to submit to Manchu laws and customs. Many Chinese did not submit willingly. The Manchus created the Qing dynasty, which controlled China until 1911. The Qing emperors—

following Chinese tradition—were said to have divine authority to rule, the so-called *tian ming,* or "Mandate of Heaven."

When Deng was born in 1904, the Manchu rulers faced internal rebellion. Discontented religious leaders with peasant armies, secret societies that concealed their defiance of Manchu law, and powerful warlords who fought for territorial control all threatened the Qing dynasty.

In addition to defending itself against national uprisings, China's imperial government also had to defend itself against foreign invasions. Russia, Japan, France, Britain, and Germany all attacked China during the nineteenth century and established their own colonies. The Europeans and Japanese dominated trade in the colonies and profited from cheap Chinese labor. Foreigners opened businesses that forced smaller Chinese businesses to close. Foreigners also built schools, clubs, churches, and factories to benefit themselves but not

Empress Dowager Cixi held imperial power at the turn of the twentieth century.

Emperor Pu Yi was the last emperor of China. The Qing dynasty collapsed in 1911, and Pu Yi was forced to give up the throne in 1912.

the Chinese. The foreigners even hung up signs that humiliated the Chinese. The signs read "No Dogs or Chinese Allowed."

The cost of fighting Chinese rebels and foreigners forced China into bankruptcy. And the infiltration of Western ideas caused many Chinese people to question traditional life under oppressive rulers. In 1911, the Qing dynasty collapsed. In February 1912, the last Manchu emperor, Pu Yi, gave up the "Mandate of Heaven" and stepped down from his throne.

In the nineteenth and early twentieth centuries, the majority of people in China were peasants at the mercy of feudal leaders. These Chinese labored all day just to earn their small bowls of grain.

Eventually the Chinese people started protesting China's outdated social system and foreign interference in China's government. In Tiananmen Square on May 4, 1919, three thousand students protested Japan's control of parts of China.

People's Republic of China
(Modern Borders)

KAZAKHSTAN

KYRGYZSTAN
TAJIKISTAN
PAKISTAN

INDIA

NEPAL

BANGLA-
DESH

BAY OF
BENGAL

BHUTAN

INDIA

MYANMAR
(BURMA)

THAI-
LAND

LAOS

VIETNAM

XIZANG (TIBET)

• Lhasa

XINJIANG

• Ürümqi

QINGHAI

GANSU

• Xining

Lanzhou •

Long March
(1934–1935)

NINGXIA

Yinchuan •

NEI MONGOL

Hohhot •

MONGOLIA

RUSSIA

(INNER MONGOLIA)

YUNNAN

Kunming •

Guiyang •

GUIZHOU

Nanning •

GUANGXI

Haikou •

HAINAN

MACAO

XIANGGANG (HONG KONG)

GUANGDONG

Guangzhou •

HUNAN

Changsha •

Chengdu •
Guang'an •
Chongqing •

Chang Jiang (Yangtze River)

SICHUAN

SHAANXI

Xi'an •

Wuqi •

HUBEI

Wuhan •

HENAN

Zhengzhou •

Huang Jiang (Yellow River)

SHANXI

Taiyuan •

Shijiazhuang •

HEBEI

Beijing,
BEIJING

★

Tianjin, TIANJIN

SHANDONG

Jinan •

ANHUI

Hefei •

JIANGSU

Nanjing •

Shanghai, SHANGHAI •

EAST
CHINA
SEA

Yudu •
Ruijin •

JIANGXI

Nanchang •

Fuzhou •

FUJIAN

ZHEJIANG

Hangzhou •

Taipei ★

TAIWAN

SOUTH
CHINA
SEA

PACIFIC OCEAN

N →

LIAONING

Shenyang •

JILIN

Changchun •

Harbin •

HEILONGJIANG

NORTH
KOREA

SOUTH
KOREA

JAPAN

The protesters earned national sympathy, and their action ignited major political movements in the 1920s and 1930s.

From 1904 until 1920, Deng lived in a rural landowning family in the Guang'an County of Sichuan Province. Although he did not take part in any of China's early twentieth century political uprisings, he probably learned about them from his father, who was a local political leader. Deng went to school, prepared himself for foreign study, and then left China to live in France. Deng's six years abroad thrust him from his protected childhood into an international political movement that would change the course of China's history.

Deng Xiaoping modeled a cowboy hat at his first Texas rodeo in 1979. Deng's tour of the United States that year marked a positive turning point in Chinese-American relations.

ONE

COWBOY DENG

We're at three times the speed of sound," U.S. astronaut Fred Haise told Deng Xiaoping, China's vice premier. Deng hunched excitedly over the control panel inside a spaceship simulator.

On February 2, 1979, at the Lyndon B. Johnson Space Center in Houston, Texas, seventy-four-year-old Deng Xiaoping took off on his second simulated spaceflight. He peered through the cockpit window as astronaut Haise pointed out the simulated sights one hundred thousand feet below. The Pacific coast, glittering Las Vegas, and Edwards Air Force Base in California were projected onto a television screen. Finally Deng pushed the button to lower the ship's landing gear, and raising both arms in the air, he smiled as his ship neared the runway.

Deng was having fun on the sixth day of his tour of the United States, and he wasn't concerned about time. When his escorts announced he was behind schedule, Deng reluctantly quit before his third flight and climbed out of the spaceship. He rejoined his large entourage and headed to a Texas-style barbecue at a restaurant outside of Houston.

Deng must have been relieved to see his dinner plate that night after several days of eating roast veal and broccoli. Deng was not fond of the meals, but someone had told Deng's American hosts that the Chinese leader liked bland food. The Americans thought veal would be the perfect dish.

Texans, however, are not known for their bland food, and they served Deng spiced beef, ribs, sausages, tangy baked beans, potato salad, and jalapeño peppers. This food was quite unlike the rice and chopped meat and vegetables that the Chinese customarily eat, but Deng ate heartily. He was, after all, from Sichuan—the spicy-food capital of China.

After dinner Deng and his wife, Zhou Lin, entered a lively rodeo arena. Deng thrilled the crowd by donning a ten-gallon cowboy hat and waving. The crowd cheered Deng on as he and his foreign minister, Huang Hua, rode twice around the arena in a horse-drawn stagecoach.

Deng Xiaoping's formal tour of the United States was the first one made by a top-ranking leader of the People's Republic of China in thirty years. China and the United States had stopped trading with each other during the Korean War (1950–1953). China had supported Russian-controlled North Korea, while the United States had supported South Korea. In the 1970s, President Nixon reopened dialogue with China, and on January 1, 1979, President Jimmy Carter normalized official relations between the two countries. Deng Xiaoping's visit brought promise of new trade and technological exchange to both countries.

Deng Xiaoping and Zhou Lin had begun their official tour in Washington, D.C., on a stormy Monday morning on January 29. Stepping out of their black limousine, they received a nineteen-gun salute. President Jimmy Carter and his wife, Rosalynn, greeted them on the White House lawn.

In Washington, Deng met privately with President Carter several times. In the presidential Oval Office, Deng was confident, articulate, and in charge. Through an interpreter, he and Carter spoke easily about world unrest.

After meetings with Carter and other politicians, Deng agreed to several small pacts. The United States agreed to let China open consulates in Houston and San Francisco, and China allowed the United States the same privileges in Guangzhou and Shanghai, two major Chinese cities. The United States also agreed to sell China a communications satellite system worth five hundred million dollars and an electron-volt accelerator used in nuclear research. Both countries agreed to exchange scholars, journalists, and cultural groups. Carter and Deng claimed this was the beginning of a new relationship.

From Washington, Deng flew to Atlanta, Georgia, where he visited the grave of Martin Luther King Jr., and toured the Ford Motor Company with Henry Ford II. Then he went on to Houston and finally to Seattle, Washington, where he was anxious to see the Boeing aircraft plant at which three 747 jumbo jets were being built for China.

All along his route, Deng charmed business leaders and politicians. Although some American leaders refused to do business with a Communist country, most looked forward to warmer relations with China. As Deng was leaving the United States, he proclaimed that "the honeymoon will continue."

Deng was born in the eastern part of Sichuan Province, a vast, mainly rural area with lush green rice paddies.

TWO

ENTERING THE YEAR OF THE DRAGON

On August 22, 1904, Deng Xiaoping was born in Guang'an County, in the vast southwestern Sichuan Province. China was still ruled by the Qing dynasty seated far away in Beijing (then called Peking). Daily life in this hilly country-side was organized around farming and food gathering; birth, marriage, and death ceremonies; religious ritual; and de-fending hearth and home against menacing warlords. War-lords were local leaders who grabbed civil and military power for themselves in regions that were not closely ruled.

Deng's father was Deng Wenming, and his mother was Deng Danshi. In China the family name, Deng, comes first. The boy's father named him Xiansheng, which means "first sage." Later, a teacher suggested changing the boy's name to Deng Xixian, which means "to aspire to goodness." As was customary, the teacher's wisdom was honored, and the name was changed. Deng used this new name for twenty years, but he later took the name Deng Xiaoping. *Xiao* means "small" in Chinese, and *ping* means "peaceful" or "balanced."

Deng's parents lived a rural life in Paifeng, a village a few miles away from Guang'an, where the region's government was located. This part of China was isolated and crisscrossed with rivers and mist-covered hills. Villages were connected by footpaths, not by roads. Fields of rice, wheat, corn, and sorghum and plots of hearty vegetables provided good food.

Deng Wenming owned almost twenty-five acres on which he grew as many as ten tons of grain each year. The family had plenty to eat, and Deng Wenming employed laborers to work the farm. He also raised mules, donkeys, and cows for fieldwork, and he tended a vegetable garden.

Deng's family lived in a large half-timbered house with packed-earth floors, a thatched roof, paper-covered windows, and twenty-two rooms. The family used unadorned wooden furniture and little home decoration. As was usual in rural houses, there was no indoor plumbing and no central heating to combat the winter chill. Behind the house was a lush bamboo grove. Ducks and chickens ran loose around the house, and the family kept several geese in the courtyard. The geese were not for eating but for protection. They honked at trespassers.

Not many details of Deng's early life are recorded. Paifeng neighbors have described Deng Xiaoping as having been a happy, secure, and energetic child. He was always small for his age, and his full, round face was expressive. His widely set eyes were alert. Playing vigorously with his older sister, he was careful not to be too rough. He is said to have loved doing somersaults down village footpaths and climbing the stone archway at the village entrance.

Deng Xiaoping had seven siblings, but some of these children had different mothers. Deng Wenming had one wife and three concubines, a common practice for Chinese men at the time. His first wife died without having children. Deng's mother, Deng Danshi, was Deng Wenming's second wife.

Deng Xiaoping's parents had three boys and one girl together. Deng was the first son, born in a hand-carved and lacquered mahogany bed brought to the home by his mother.

Deng Danshi is said to have been illiterate but practical, earning family income from raising silkworms and giving advice to villagers in dispute. Deng Danshi loved her first son, but she did not see him reach manhood. She died—probably of tuberculosis—sometime in the 1920s.

Deng Xiaoping's father was not a scholar, but he had attended school. He valued education and paid close attention to local and national affairs. He was away from home frequently, serving the local government and gathering information on local and national politics. Active in a spiritual sect

Deng's birth home, above, in Paifeng is a traditional Chinese compound made up of buildings set around an open area.

called the "Religion of Five Sons" (a sect that combined Confucianism, Buddhism, and Taoism), Deng Wenming worshiped regularly at temples and went on religious pilgrimages. He was also captain of the town militia, but he secretly belonged to the Ko-lao Hui, the Elder Brothers Society.

The Elder Brothers Society was a secret association that had members in towns and villages throughout rural China. They had influential connections to the central military and to some corrupt imperial officials.

In rural China, the central government did not send officials to govern peasant families. Instead, village heads were chosen for their wealth and leadership qualities. Deng Wenming was selected as the head of the Paifeng village. He made sure peasants paid their taxes, and he reported serious crimes.

Deng Wenming is said to have wanted China to reform and modernize politically and socially. Imperial rule was feudal rule with the emperor and his family at the top of society, selected nobles at a privileged rank just below, and most of China's people living impoverished and powerless lives. Deng Wenming wanted his children to have a broad education and learn more than Confucian philosophy.

Deng Xiaoping's early school records cannot be verified, but several of his schoolmates remembered him as brilliant, playful, and mischievous. Others said his work was mediocre. Friends said he was a good son, never a rebel.

In 1909 when Deng Xiaoping was five, his father hired a private tutor trained in Confucian classics. Using a simple phrase book and a book of clan names, a few male pupils (no female students attended) were introduced to written Chinese characters and Confucian thought. A year later, Deng was sent off to a primary school, where he was taught to memorize and recite passages from Confucian texts. Neatly dressed in silks and satins, carrying lunches of fried rice and steamed wheat buns, Deng was the promising son.

In 1915 when Deng Xiaoping was eleven years old, he attended a higher level primary school in Guang'an County as a boarding student. The teaching method at this school was similar to that of his last school—memorization and recitation. Once a week, Deng walked stone paths and climbed hills to return for a night with his family.

In 1919 at age fourteen, Deng switched schools again and finally began to study mathematics, geography, and science along with the classics at the Guang'an County Middle School. He did not stay there long, however.

After reading a newspaper notice about a new preparatory school in Chongqing, Deng Wenming suggested to his much younger brother, Deng Shaosheng, and to his first son that they enter this school. The purpose of the new school was to prepare students for a work-study program in France.

There are no records stating why Deng Wenming wanted his son to go to France, but some Chinese were inspired by France's economic and political movements. Communism was gaining French support. The Chinese also believed that France was a country of new scientific discoveries. Many Chinese saw their own educational system—based on Confucian texts—as old-fashioned. They believed young Chinese needed to understand modern technology, international trade laws, modern mathematical and scientific theories, and industrial planning.

Deng Wenming had to sell some of his rice fields to pay for his son's tuition and steamship ticket to France. In late summer or early fall of 1919, Deng Xiaoping and his uncle, Deng Shaosheng, began attending the new preparatory school in Chongqing.

Deng posed for a photograph on his way to France at age 16.

THREE

POLITICAL AWAKENING

The Chongqing school enrolled more than one hundred students, who were divided into an elementary group and an advanced group. Deng studied a broader range of subjects than he had studied before. The courses included French, algebra, geometry, physics, and Chinese.

Deng's schoolwork was modest. He did not earn top grades. French was particularly challenging for him. Even simple French phrases often stumped him. On his final examinations, however, he did well enough to go on to France—but not well enough to earn a full scholarship.

After finishing his courses, Deng went home to pack his belongings and say good-bye to his family before leaving for France. On the night before his departure, Deng's father took him aside for a private discussion. Deng Wenming asked his son what the boy hoped to learn in France. Deng Xiaoping thought, and then he repeated words he had learned from his teachers: "To learn knowledge and truth from the West in order to save China." Deng Xiaoping had been taught that China was weak and poor and that the Chinese people must have a modern, Western education to save their country.

Deng Wenming nodded at his son and quizzed him further about an important quote from Confucius. Deng Xiaoping began reciting the requested phrase and his father finished it: "To take good care of the state, one should first of all take good care of himself. He would be a sage who could fulfill both objectives." Obviously his son's well-being and future were as important to Deng Wenming as was the future of China. He wanted his son to know that.

At three o'clock in the afternoon on August 27, 1920, Deng Xiaoping—the youngest in the group—and about eighty other students from the Chongqing preparatory school set sail on a steamer, the *Jiqing,* for Shanghai. His journey to Shanghai took eight days. After spending a week in Shanghai, Deng Xiaoping and almost two hundred other students boarded the *André Lebon* bound for France on September 11, 1920. The next thirty-nine days were not easy sailing.

The Chinese students traveled fourth class, which meant they had to sleep on the ship's top open deck or in the suffocating cargo hold below. The deck was windy and wet, and the cargo hold was full of bugs. Because they were not allowed into the dining room, the students had to make their skimpy meals wherever they found space. Many students suffered terrible seasickness and homesickness. Some of them even got off the ship at Asian ports because they could not bear the travel conditions.

If Deng Xiaoping felt sick or unhappy at sea, he did not reveal this fact publicly. If anything, he showed tolerance and lack of emotion. Being the youngest of the Chinese students, he had to prove himself worthy of their respect.

Deng and his fellow students arrived in Marseilles—a Mediterranean port city in southern France—on October 19, 1920. They were relieved to put their feet on firm ground and to meet representatives of the Sino-Franco Society of Education (SFSE). That same day, the students boarded a bus that took them from Marseilles to Paris. Sixteen hours later, they reached Paris, where hundreds of other Chinese students and workers were already living.

The new Chinese students were separated into groups of about twenty. Each group was sent to a different provincial secondary school. Deng and his uncle—dressed in Western suits and ties—went to a secondary school in Bayeux, a city in the Normandy region of France.

Although he was optimistic about acquiring knowledge that would be useful back in China, Deng did not like his situation at the Bayeux Middle School. He claimed that the school treated the Chinese students like children, made them go to bed early in the dormitories, and taught them very little. He also complained about the school's food.

The Chinese students in Deng's program were told they would study French first. When they became proficient in the language, they could take other secondary school courses.

The SFSE was not as organized or as well funded as the students had thought. When the program began at the end of World War I (1914–1918), France needed industrial laborers. The arrival of the Chinese work-study students was well timed. Two years later, however, French industries went through a financial crisis, and millions of people lost their jobs. The high unemployment severely affected unskilled foreign laborers.

In January 1921, the SFSE told its students that the program was out of funding. The association issued two notices announcing that it would cut off financial aid to the students after March 15, 1921. The Chinese students found themselves stranded.

Poor students who had relied on the school program for food and housing found themselves without either, and they had no money for further courses. They had to find work right away. The Chinese began competing with each other for jobs. Fewer than three hundred students—out of a total of fifteen hundred—were hired.

Even with employment, the Chinese students suffered. They took on factory work or they pulled vegetable and milk carts to market at night, loaded and unloaded baggage at train stations, polished shoes, peeled potatoes in restaurant kitchens, laid bricks, or collected garbage.

The former students lived in grim dormitories owned by factories or in cheap boardinghouses. They soon learned that their bosses wanted the most work out of the Chinese while paying the lowest possible wages—sometimes half the rate earned by French workers. Some of the poorest Chinese died from hunger, illness, or exposure to workplace chemicals.

Deng Xiaoping had family funds, so he was not immediately desperate. Instead of finding a place at another school, however, he chose to accompany his uncle and seventeen penniless Chinese students to a company called Schneider & Company Iron and Steel Complex located between Paris and Lyons. Deng began work on April 2, 1921.

At age sixteen, Deng quickly learned firsthand about hard labor and dismal workplace conditions. Company records show that Deng transferred hot metal plates and bars from a conveyer belt to different places in the shop—for fifty or more hours per week. The rolled steel bars or plates could weigh as much as two hundred pounds, and the temperature in the workshop was usually above one hundred degrees Fahrenheit.

Sometimes the steel bars flew off the belts and hit

workers, seriously injuring them. At other times, workers fell off the rolling belts and severely burned themselves. Workers were often made to labor overtime on night shifts. They had little rest, and they paid for their own food and work clothes. Deng lasted three weeks at this job. He decided he would rather take his chances in Paris—looking for a new job and school program—than remain under the conditions at Schneider.

Deng left for Paris on April 23, 1921, and moved to a Chinese community in La Garenne-Colombes, a suburb of Paris. Living in a neighborhood of Chinese immigrants, Deng quickly learned how to get by in France on meager funds and poor French language skills.

Over the next four and a half years abroad, Deng lived in low-income housing, factory dormitories, or cheap hotels. He was able to afford only three more months of schooling, during the winter of 1922–1923. When he ran out of family money, he had to look for another job. Instead of studying, he labored as a factory worker, a locomotive fireman, a restaurant kitchen helper, and as an unskilled worker at Renault, the French car manufacturer.

In France, Deng did not acquire as much knowledge of modern technology or science as he and his father had hoped. However, later in life he claimed that he learned another important lesson that he did not appreciate until he was older. "In the first two years, I got an initial feel for the evils of the capitalist society. But with romantic ideas about life, I could not have a profound understanding."

While in France, Deng soaked up the foreign lifestyle and imitated French habits. He became fond of eating potatoes, croissants, bread, and cheese and drinking wine and coffee—when he had enough money to buy these treats. Deng also bought cheap tickets to soccer matches and learned to play bridge and cricket.

In addition to learning about European culture, Deng learned about politics and public demonstrations. On February 21, 1921, three hundred Chinese students demonstrated outside the Chinese Embassy in Paris. They shouted at Ambassador Chen Lu, reminding him of the promises of the work-study program to educate and find decent employment for Chinese students. Finally the Chinese ambassador promised small funds for all unemployed Chinese students.

This promise calmed the demonstrators but did not solve the problem of education. A second demonstration took place in Lyons, where the program administrators accepted only those students from rich families who could pay their full tuition. This time 125 demonstrating Chinese students were arrested by the French police and detained for two months in army barracks. The French did not want the Chinese to cause trouble in their streets. Almost all the students were deported back to China.

Although Deng did not participate in these demonstrations, he did sign a petition to the Chinese Embassy requesting admission to Lyons University for all the work-study students. Clearly, he understood the situation and knew students who had organized the demonstrations.

Deng finally reached a dead end. On June 11, 1923, he gave up hope of ever earning enough to study in France. From that point on, he turned his energies toward helping his colleagues. He decided that working for social justice was more important than taking more French classes.

In France in the 1920s, the Socialist and Communist parties were powerful political groups trying to change the French government. Influenced by the Russian Revolution of

1917—in which Communist workers took over the central government and gave land and power to the people—French workers and citizens questioned their own ruling system. They often banded together and demonstrated in the streets. The different groups were often at odds with each other over how to help the poor and weaken the powerful. Political infighting was common. Some activists demonstrated violently and were arrested. Much of their work had to be done "underground," hidden from the government and police.

Many Chinese students were influenced by the French Communist activities. They began to read Communist theory—particularly the theory developed by the German thinker Karl Marx—and to study how the Russians had overthrown their oppressive czar.

Deng Xiaoping was one of those who examined Marxist literature. He soon began discussing political ideas with the Chinese student leaders around him. Later in life, Deng explained his first exposure to Communist thought. "From my working experience, with the help of fellow progressive students and under the influence of the French workers' movement, I started to make changes in my ideology. I began to read some Marxist works and attend some meetings at which some Chinese or French propagated communism. Then I also wanted to join revolutionary organizations."

During the second half of Deng's stay in France—late 1923 to early 1926—Deng worked with Chinese students who had been writing articles about Communism and holding meetings to spread Communist ideas. One of the more experienced students, Zhou Enlai, befriended Deng. Beginning in January 1924, Deng worked in Zhou's room in a cheap residential hotel. This was the secret publication office of the Communist Youth League, a group of young Communists that had formed on June 3, 1922. Since June of 1923, the group had been publishing a journal about Communism called *Red Lights*. Zhou and Deng put together this journal and other handouts on Communism. Zhou was well aware of the growing Communist movement in China, and Deng learned a great deal from him.

Deng's first job with Zhou included typing, copying, and typesetting articles for *Red Lights*. Because he was so enthusiastic and careful in copying articles, Deng was soon given the nickname "Doctor of Mimeography." By the end of 1924, Deng had become a member of the Communist Youth League and had begun writing his own articles for the league's newsletter. Later he became one of the editors.

Zhou Enlai and several of the other Chinese Communist leaders left France in 1924 to join the growing political revolution in China. As the senior leaders departed, Deng moved up in the ranks. By the end of 1925, he had become one of the senior political planners. Although enthusiastic, Deng was not a skilled or eloquent writer or speaker. His understanding of Communist ideology was not deep. However, Deng was an energetic demonstrator whose spirit attracted others.

Because Deng became such an active political worker, the French police opened a file on him. They wanted to rid France of the Communist activists who broke laws and carried out dangerous political activities against the government. The French police learned Deng's name and followed him. They sent spies to the Chinese meetings and recorded things he said and did. According to French police records, Deng did not break any French laws. They could not arrest him. However, they decided to raid Deng Xiaoping's residence on the outskirts of Paris to hunt for proof of Deng's unauthorized political activities.

Deng worked closely with Zhou Enlai in France and later in China. Zhou, shown here in 1934, and Deng helped put together Red Lights, *a Communist journal.*

At 5:45 on the morning of January 8, 1926, the police entered Deng's room. Inside they found many French and Chinese booklets promoting Communism, some printing equipment, and packs of printing paper. But they did not find what they really wanted. Deng Xiaoping was gone.

Documents reveal that Deng and his colleagues had planned to leave Paris before the police raid. A paper dated January 7, 1926, clearly stated, "Twenty-one of our comrades are scheduled to leave Paris for Moscow this very night. They will soon return to the motherland, comrades!"

On January 7, 1926, when Deng was twenty-one years old, he boarded a train to Berlin, Germany, and then continued on to Moscow. French police were glad to be rid of Deng.

Dr. Sun Yatsen hoped to establish a republic of China. He was a leader in the Nationalist movement in the early 1900s and strove for unification of China until the time of his death in 1925.

FOUR

As Political
Commanding Officer

When Deng Xiaoping and his Communist Youth
League colleagues arrived in Moscow, they were welcomed
by other Chinese students already living and studying there.
Deng entered the Soviet Union's Eastern University, which
was set up and funded by the government to educate and train
national and international students. The faculty taught Communist theory and political campaigning tactics. Deng was inspired by such an educational purpose. He was ready to learn
more about Communism, and he formally became a member
of the Chinese Communist Party (CCP).

Later in life Deng explained, "When I came to Moscow, I
had already made up my mind to give my whole life to our
Party and our class more resolutely. Henceforth, I am ready
to absolutely receive the Party's training, obey the Party's
command, and always fight for the interests of the proletariat
[the working class]."

All the Chinese students who went to Moscow before
1926 studied at the Eastern University. In contrast to the situation in France, the students in Moscow were given room,
board, clothing, medical care, and even entertainment. Deng

studied for a few months at the Eastern University and then transferred to the Sun Yatsen University.

Sun Yatsen University was set up in 1926 to train both Chinese Communists and Chinese Nationalists, who were fighting together in China against the warlords. At that time, neither the Communist Party nor the Nationalist Party was well defined in terms of membership or politics. Supporters in one party worked with supporters in the other.

The Chinese students at the Sun Yatsen University studied subjects such as the history of the Communist Party, the history of Chinese and East Asian revolutions, and the Russian language. They also took military training. The teachers lectured, encouraged free discussion, and invited famous leaders of the Russian Revolution to talk to the Chinese students. The students hoped to become leaders of a Chinese Communist revolution. Deng became the head of his class's Chinese Communist Party group, and he temporarily adopted the Russian name Dozorov. Because of his short but sturdy size, his peers also gave him the nickname "Little Cannon."

According to Sun Yatsen University records, Deng was recommended for future work organizing and spreading information about Communist activities. He earned only modest grades but was an enthusiastic young Communist.

In late 1926, Chinese Communist Party officials chose Deng and about twenty other Chinese students in the Soviet Union to teach Communist ideology in China. Deng Xiaoping, at age twenty-two, left Moscow by train and arrived in Ulan Bator, Mongolia, in early 1927. Deng and two other students then traveled across the Gobi Desert in Soviet trucks carrying ammunition. Before their journey was over, they had to ride camels and horses to reach Xi'an, in northern China, in March 1927.

Deng's assignment was to teach in Feng Yuxiang's army in northwest China. Feng was a warlord who began supporting the Nationalist movement in China, and he received political backing from the Soviet government. Deng began teaching Feng's soldiers the Communist theory and political strategies that he had learned in Moscow, but his new job did not last long.

In April 1927, the Chinese Nationalists, led by Chiang Kaishek, ended their alliance with the Communists. Feng Yuxiang sided with the Nationalists, and this political move caused problems for Deng. Party boundaries were ambiguous, and many people sided with the most powerful group of the moment. Although Chiang Kaishek ordered the murder of thousands of Communists, Feng Yuxiang peacefully purged the Communists from his army.

Deng left Feng's military offices in Xi'an and went to Wuhan, in central China, where the Communist Party Center was located. There the Party was in chaos because of the threat of attack by Nationalist soldiers. Party leadership soon disbanded as a result of the fighting, but a temporary committee of five men quickly reorganized it. Among the new leaders were Zhou Enlai and two of Deng's other acquaintances from France.

Deng served as a record keeper and staff member. To obscure his identity for security reasons, he changed his name from Deng Xixian—the name his first teacher had given him—to Deng Xiaoping. In Wuhan, Deng met Mao Zedong, who was a popular and highly recognized Communist Party member. At that time, however, they did not work together. Deng soon moved with the party officers to Shanghai, where they relocated their central office in order to hide from the Nationalists. Although their new center was in Shanghai, the

Mao Zedong, shown here in 1933, was an inspiring speaker and soldier for the Chinese Communist Party.

Communists did not have control of the city. They had to do all their political campaigning underground, secretly.

For the next three years, Deng worked wherever the Party sent him. He did underground work as a secretary. Later, Deng became political trainer to the Party's Seventh Army. In this job, he taught basic Communist ideology, watched for signs of disloyalty among party members, and reported any betrayal.

In early 1928, Deng Xiaoping married a young woman, Zhang Xiyuan, whom he had first met in Moscow. Born in 1907, Zhang was a soft-spoken and friendly woman from Peking. She was barely nineteen years old when she went to Moscow for training at the Sun Yatsen University. Like Deng, she left Moscow to do underground work for the Communist movement. To hide their Communist activities, Deng and Zhang posed as shopkeepers.

The couple was said to be very close and affectionate, but they were married for only two years. Some accounts state that when Deng was away on a mission and had no contact with his wife, Zhang died during the birth of their child. However, conflicting sources indicate that Deng did see his wife in the Baolong Hospital in Shanghai and was there when she contracted a fever and died. The couple's baby girl died a few days later.

At twenty-six, Deng Xiaoping became a widower. He grieved quietly but could not attend the funeral of his wife and

Chiang Kaishek led the Nationalist Party in China from 1927 to 1949. Under Chiang's leadership, the Nationalists broke ties with the Communists.

child because of the urgent and secretive nature of his work as a party secretary. This was a hectic and frightening period for Chinese Communists. Many of the Communists who were not arrested or killed by the Nationalists committed suicide or deserted. Distrust was widespread.

By the end of 1928, the Nationalist Guomindang army under Chiang Kaishek seemed to have defeated or reformed most of the powerful warlords in China. Chiang then set up a central government in Nanjing and promised to build a unified China. Chiang adopted Western technology, medicine, communication systems, and a unified currency system. But he did little to upgrade the lives of the poor peasants or the

Thousands of Chinese gathered at Communist rallies in the 1920s and 1930s to support the Chinese Communist Party.

urban laborers who worked long hours for little pay. Many peasants did not trust Chiang.

The Communists had not given up their fight to take over China, and Chiang knew that. The Communists spread into rural villages and small, poverty-stricken cities to teach people that they did not have to live under oppressive conditions. The Communists taught the poorly educated Chinese to demand land, food, and tax reduction in their villages. The villagers began supporting the Communists.

Deng's next assignment was to go to Guangxi Province to coordinate local Communists in an armed uprising against the provincial government allied with Chiang Kaishek. Deng's mission was successful, and he became the local Communist Party representative.

By November 1930, Deng became the secretary of the Seventh Red Army. (The Communist army called itself the Red Army.) After losing battles to the Nationalists in Guangxi Province, the Seventh Red Army was unable to attack cities in southern China. Instead, it turned northeast to join the large Jiangxi Communist military base that controlled the Jiangxi Province.

Because the Seventh Army had originally planned to go south to a warm climate, the soldiers were unprepared for marching northward. Soon their mission was just to survive. Walking long distances in snow and ice, the exhausted soldiers—Deng Xiaoping among them—had nothing to wear but thin sleeveless vests and straw sandals. Several died from the cold. When local Nationalist soldiers found and attacked the weakened Seventh Army, half of the remaining soldiers died or suffered serious injury.

At that point in the Communist fight against the Nationalists, Deng was desperate. The troop to which he was attached was now severely weakened. His job as political trainer seemed useless. Sometime in early March 1931, Deng left the Communist army to make his way back to the Shanghai Party Center. What happened there exactly is still unclear, but Chinese military records indicate that Deng's departure had not been authorized by his superiors. His act was seen as desertion.

On April 29, 1931, Deng submitted a Seventh Army battle report to the Party Center in Shanghai. He explained the failure of the Seventh Army but took only partial responsibility. His job was political trainer, not military commander. He was not executed as some of the other Seventh Army officers were, but Zhou Enlai may have shielded him. This desertion was, nevertheless, a black mark on his career.

In the late summer of 1931, Deng made his way from Shanghai to the central base area of Jiangxi. This area—ten thousand miles of mountainous countryside on both sides of the Jiangxi and Fujian border—was well established as Communist territory. There the Communists set up military, party, and government offices that worked together to control the region economically and politically. They were successful in that region because they brought peasants into the local governments, taught the people how to vote in regional elections, and carried out land reform that gave the peasants land to grow food.

Land reform was the process of taking land from wealthy landlords—often by violent and bloody force—and giving it to the peasants. In theory, land reform was an effective way to help the poor. In practice, it was often terrifying. Workers and peasants felt politically justified in attacking landlords and taking over their homes and property.

Mao Zedong was the main leader at the Jiangxi base area.

However, he often argued with other Communist leaders over military tactics. The party control kept changing, and this created a weakened military situation. Chiang Kaishek hoped to take advantage of this weakness, and he tried unsuccessfully to overtake the region four times.

Over the next three years, Deng Xiaoping held many positions in the ever-shifting Communist military units. He was slowly promoted up the ranks.

In the summer of 1932, Deng married again. His new bride, Jin Weiying—commonly called Ah Jin—was also a party member. However, she was not loyal to Deng. A year after the marriage, when Deng came under political attack for supporting Mao's war strategies that were unpopular with some Communist leaders, Ah Jin left Deng. She went off with his chief accuser, Li Weihan.

Deng was alone for the second time. He was forced to write self-criticisms for supporting Mao, and he was given a serious warning by party officials who were unsure if they could trust him. Sometime in the summer of 1933, Deng was reassigned. He became editor of the *Red Star,* a weekly Communist newspaper.

In October 1933, Chiang Kaishek attempted a fifth attack on the Communist base area. This time he sent out more than one million soldiers to wipe out the Communists in the Jiangxi region. Using new military tactics to choke off the base, Chiang progressed steadily and pushed the Communists into a desperate retreat.

On October 15, 1934, the Long March—the year-long Communist army retreat—officially began. Eighty thousand Communist soldiers, fifteen thousand government and party officials, and thirty-five women, most of whom were wives of the leaders or supporters, were in the retreating party.

Deng Xiaoping was one of the Long Marchers. Having been promoted by Zhou Enlai and Mao Zedong to the position of general secretary to the Communist Party's Central Committee, he became one of the members of the party's operating center. Deng and Mao were often together during the treacherous retreat.

For the next year, the marchers tramped more than seventeen miles each day, crossed twenty-four rivers and eighteen mountain ranges. Altogether they covered more than six thousand miles of harsh landscape. They could not stop for long because the Nationalists were never far behind.

With little food and tattered clothing, the marchers had nothing but their spirit to help them survive. When their few horses died, the marchers ate horse meat. When they reached unpopulated grasslands, they ate grass roots and tree bark. And when they crossed completely barren plateaus, they even gnawed on belt leather.

Deng was stricken with typhoid fever and was close to death at the end of the march. By the time they reached Yan'an in northern China in the fall of 1935, the number of Long Marchers had been reduced by 95 percent. The self-sacrifice and camaraderie of the troops toward the rural peasants also won the Long Marchers a place as national heroes.

The Communists set up a new base and lived in caves in the remote Shaanxi Province. There, Deng Xiaoping resumed his duties as a party secretary and *Red Star* editor. The Communists reorganized leadership that had been divided before and during the march. Mao Zedong came out the victor. Mao, Zhou, and Deng worked well together during this period, and Deng was given several important political jobs over the next two years.

With Japan's 1937 invasion of China—marking the start

of World War II in Asia—Mao Zedong made a national call to unite Communists and Nationalists to fight off the Japanese. Chiang Kaishek did not want to risk losing his troops in Japanese attacks. He wanted to save his soldiers for fighting the Communists. The Japanese advanced viciously. The attacks forced a cease-fire between the Communists and Nationalists, finally creating a united Chinese effort against Japan.

When the Japanese took Beijing, Tianjin, Shanghai, and then killed two hundred thousand Chinese in Nanking, the Chinese people became desperate. The Japanese motto was to kill all, burn all, and destroy all. Instead of fighting back, Chiang Kaishek retreated inland. The Chinese people were angered and humiliated by Japan's dominance and Chiang's weakness. The Communists, however, stepped in to counterattack Japanese armies. This led many Chinese to support the Communists.

In September 1937, Deng Xiaoping was appointed deputy director of the political department of the Eighth Route Army. He was a document handler and received secret military telegrams. From September 1937 until January 1938, Deng lived in Buddhist monasteries and temples in the Wutai Mountains.

In January 1938, Mao promoted Deng to the position of political commissar of the 129th Division of the Eighth Route Army. Deng trained soldiers in Communist theory and strategy, wrote political articles, and gave speeches about the military and economic affairs of the Communist Party.

The Red Army's 129th Division was under the military command of Liu Bocheng, a popular leader with whom Deng worked very closely. The two men established army bases in the Taihang Mountains and expanded their troops from six thousand to thirteen thousand soldiers. Their soldiers carried

In the 1930s and 1940s, Deng rose through the ranks of the Communist Party.

out counterattacks on local Nationalist armies. Deng and Liu's troops secured a Communist hold in northern China.

Mao often called Deng to Yan'an to attend Communist Party conferences. Deng became a strong liaison between the 129th Division and the Party Central Committee. He spent much time in Mao's private cave discussing party politics and theory. During this period, Mao developed much of his own political thought, which later became the basis of Chinese Communist Party education and government. Deng became devoted to Mao, and a mutual respect developed.

During a July 1939 stay in Yan'an, Deng met and married Zhou Lin, a recent college graduate who had majored in physics at the Normal University for Women in Beijing. After college, Zhou Lin had left the capital city and gone to Yan'an to work with the growing Communist Party. Both Mao and Zhou Enlai attended Deng's third wedding, and the newlywed couple soon returned to Deng's army base in the mountains. Unlike several other young women who married Communist Party leaders, Zhou Lin became more interested in family life than in politics. She gave birth to a girl, Deng Lin, in 1941, and a boy, Deng Pufang, in 1943.

From 1941 until 1945, Deng worked as one of the few senior Communist leaders in northern China. He gained respect for his work with Liu's army, which had expanded and held out against both Nationalist and Japanese attacks in the northern province. At the Seventh Congress of the Chinese Communist Party in Yan'an, party members elected Deng as a high-ranking member of the Party Central Committee. Deng was a proven Mao supporter.

*In 1945 the U.S. Army exploded atomic bombs over Nagasaki,
above, and Hiroshima, Japan. The destruction ended World War II.*

FIVE

FROM ARMY CAMP TO POLITICAL OFFICE

In August 1945, at the end of World War II, the United States Army dropped two atomic bombs on Japan. These attacks killed hundreds of thousands of Japanese, causing Japan to surrender on August 14, 1945. The Japanese were then forced to pull their troops from foreign territories, including China. The Chinese people were relieved to see their foreign oppressors depart, but China was still in a state of upheaval. The country was weakened from war and politically unstable.

In China, both the Communists and the Nationalists wanted to represent China in accepting the Japanese surrender. Although they had united somewhat to fight Japan, each side wanted control of China. Mao and Chiang sent orders out to their respective generals to prepare for new battles.

Mao dispatched soldiers to take over the formerly Japanese controlled area of Manchuria and to seize Japanese weapons. The Communists were stationed closer to the Japanese in northern China, so they had an advantage. The Nationalists knew they could not beat the Communists to the task, so they requested help from the U.S. Army, which remained in Asia after World War II.

Because the U.S. government disapproved of Communism as a political system, it sided with Chiang Kaishek and supported peace negotiations between Mao and Chiang. U.S. military planes airlifted Nationalist leaders to northern China and instructed the Japanese to surrender only to the Nationalists. The Japanese surrendered as commanded, and Mao and Chiang had to negotiate peace.

China had become bankrupt, and few Chinese wanted another war. Most wanted a solid government that could stabilize the country. Deng, however, was one of the few who wanted the Communists to continue fighting the Nationalists. He believed that only military dominance—not peace negotiations—would win Communist control of China. He also believed that Mao really wanted immediate military action against the Nationalists, and gaining Mao's respect was Deng's strongest motivation. Deng and Liu ordered their army into battle.

From August 27 until October 10, 1945, Mao and Chiang argued over political and military issues. In a written agreement, Mao accepted the legitimacy of the Nationalist central government. Chiang recognized the Chinese Communist Party as a legitimate opposition party. But these agreements were on paper only. Neither leader planned to work in a multiparty system.

On September 10, 1945—while Mao was still in peace negotiations—Deng and Liu led their troops into heavy fighting against the Nationalists in Shandong. By early October, Deng and Liu's forces had captured the city of Changzhi, wiped out thirty-five thousand Nationalist troops, captured a dozen generals, and taken control of several cities.

Deng and Liu carried out successful military strategies and fought regional battles for the next three years. They moved their troops eastward, southward, and into central China, capturing and destroying more than they lost. Before they were done, they had broken through many Nationalist blockades, expanded their army, and moved into the Dabei Mountains. Taking control of this mountainous region of China was a turning point for the Communists. Their military tactics shifted from defensive actions to offensive actions, and Deng and Liu's army took in hundreds of thousands of surrendering Nationalist troops. Their actions earned them respect from their soldiers and local peasants as well as high praise from Mao and other political officers.

By 1948 the Nationalist forces were losing momentum. Their armies were collapsing on all fronts, and they were bankrupt. The Communists had used guerrillas—roving bands of fighters who torment the enemy with ambushes, sudden raids, and other small-scale attacks—to surprise and

In an effort to gain control of cities and regions, Nationalists hike through Manchuria, an area occupied by the Japanese until 1945.

outwit the Nationalists, who had concentrated on holding big cities. The Communists also carried out radical land, rent, and tax control, which won the support of villagers. After decades of strife, Mao Zedong became the undisputed leader of China.

On October 1, 1949, in Beijing, Mao declared the establishment of the People's Republic of China, and he became its chairman. In front of millions of excited and tearful supporters in Tiananmen Square, Mao shouted into a loudspeaker. He told his supporters that China's Communist takeover was a just cause for the people and that a just cause is invincible. The masses in China believed and supported him. On that October day, Mao's piercing, high-pitched voice broadcast over Tiananmen Square brought deafening cheers. People threw confetti and hung large photos of Mao everywhere. They paraded for hours. Bands played patriotic songs. The atmosphere was jubilant, and Deng was there. As one of Mao's re-

The Nationalist Army captured these Communist soldiers in Suzhou Province in 1948, the year before the Communists gained control of China.

spected political officers, Deng could share in the triumph. His troops had helped defeat the Nationalist government. On that day, October 1, Deng wrote, "Remember forever that the victory of today was won with the blood of the people's heroes in the long and difficult years of the past."

After the declaration of the People's Republic of China, Deng and Liu returned to the south. Deng and Liu led an army into Chongqing, where Chiang Kaishek and his government had headquarters, and seized full control from the Nationalists. Ten days later, Chiang—who had fled to the island of Taiwan—announced the establishment of his government in Taipei, the capital city.

Parades across China, like this one in Shanghai, demonstrated the Chinese Communist Party's victory over the Nationalists in 1949. Party Chairman Mao Zedong and General Zhu De are portrayed on large placards on the trucks.

Deng Xiaoping then became mayor of Chongqing. He resettled his growing family—a third baby, Deng Nan, had been born in 1949—and stayed in the city for the next three years. During this time, Zhou Lin gave birth to a fourth baby, Deng Rong (called Deng Mao Mao), and to their fifth and last child, Deng Zhifang. Deng thrived as head of his busy household, and at work he took on more political rather than military responsibilities. He established Communist law and order in the city and surrounding region—setting up financial administrations, suppressing reactionary political groups, and carrying out land reform.

Deng Xiaoping's own family in Guang'an County suddenly became targets of the land reform movement. Deng called his younger brother, Deng Shuping, and instructed him to bring family members from Guang'an to Deng's headquarters as quickly as possible. Deng Shuping had been a former department chief in the Nationalist county government, so he was considered an enemy. Deng's elder sister, a younger brother, and several in-laws avoided attack by escaping into Deng Xiaoping's new government quarters.

Deng was in charge of the southwest region of China, which included five provinces—Sichuan, Guizhou, Yunnan, Xikang (which was ethnically Tibetan and incorporated in 1956 into Sichuan Province), and—according to Chinese, not Tibetan, maps—the Autonomous Region of Tibet. These areas were mainly populated by ethnic minority groups that resented central Chinese government intervention and control.

Mao's plan for 1950 was to "liberate all China," which in his mind included Tibet, Taiwan, and a few islands off China's southeastern coast. He assigned the task of conquering these areas to his trusted generals. Deng's job was to invade and—to use Mao's word—"liberate" Tibet.

Tibet had a long history of relations with the Mongol and then the Manchu emperors who had once controlled China. When Pu Yi, the last Manchu emperor of China, stepped down in 1912, Tibet declared its full independence and abandoned former ties with China. Tibet did not want Han Chinese—who were ethnically and religiously different from Tibetans—to interfere in the Tibetan government.

The Chinese, however, wanted Tibet to be an integral part of China. They wanted to control the borders with Burma, Nepal, and India and to use the underdeveloped land and resources (including gems and minerals) in Tibet. Thus, Deng planned to invade Tibet and bring it under Chinese jurisdiction. He hoped to impose Communist principles of land redistribution and state control of industry and farming on Tibet. Deng also planned to abolish Tibet's powerful religious institution—a branch of Buddhism.

In 1950 Deng ordered his troops to invade. Tibet, a remote land with no modern army or technology, was no match for China's army. Tibetan patriots fought desperately but were easily defeated.

China broadcast that it was "liberating" Tibetans peacefully from their feudal landowners, religious leaders, and foreign imperialist influence. Mao promised that as soon as Tibet could implement the Communist system, the Chinese would leave. In a speech that Deng made in July 1950, he claimed that Tibetans were "delighted with their own liberation." Tibetan reports solidly refuted Deng's statement.

Throughout the 1950s, Deng's troops killed hundreds of thousands of Tibetans. They also destroyed Tibet's beloved monasteries and temples and its social, political, and religious structures. Deng's military heads were soon dispatched to negotiate peace with Tibet's young political and spiritual leader,

Tibetans paraded through Lhasa, the capital of the province of Tibet, in 1951, following the arrival of Chinese Communist Party troops in the region. They carry Chinese flags past what was then the Dalai Lama's residence, the Potala Palace.

the Fourteenth Dalai Lama. At first the Dalai Lama thought that perhaps Communism could help Tibet modernize its government and save its poor. However, when the Dalai Lama heard reports of the violence and destruction that the Chinese had caused, he realized that Communist tactics in Tibet were muderous and shocking.

In July 1952, Deng and his family—his wife, stepmother, three daughters, and two sons—moved to Beijing, the center of Communist power. They settled into a residence near the Communist Party Center compound, Zhongnanhai. Deng's work as a military commander gave way to work as a political administrator. He gained the official title of deputy premier of the State Administrative Council. He also earned membership on several government committees with lofty titles, but his jobs did not involve much work or responsibility at first. At forty-eight years old, Deng waited for a position of real political importance.

The Fourteenth Dalai Lama met with Deng Xiaoping in 1954. At that time, the Dalai Lama was in Beijing trying to hold talks with Mao and the Communist government. He went there with an open mind toward the Communist leaders. He had hoped to prevent any more violence in Tibet. Later, he gave his impression of Deng Xiaoping: "When I was in China during 1954 [and] 1955, I met [Deng] a number of times and had been very impressed by him . . . . I heard much about him—particularly that he was a man of great ability and very decisive too."

When negotiations broke down between the Chinese and the Tibetans in March 1959, the Dalai Lama secretly escaped from his palace in Lhasa and moved his government into exile in India. In his autobiography, the Dalai Lama also called Deng a powerful and wise man. Others have called Deng feisty, impulsive, temperamental, and even cruel. Deng was notorious for his hot temper. He exploded if his commands were not carried out. He was not afraid to use violence, as when he attacked Nationalists during peace negotiations and when he attacked Tibetans, who had no national army. More than once Deng has been quoted as saying he was not afraid of bloodshed for a just cause—and Communism was a just cause, in his opinion.

In the 1950s, China's economy needed to be revived quickly. The new Communist government took control of the banks, and within a year the high costs of food and goods were brought under control. Some privately owned businesses still functioned, but landlords and company owners were publicly criticized and accused of bribery, tax evasion, or abuse of laborers. If a merchant confessed under social pressure, he was forced to pay fines to the government. This usually meant giving up his business. In this way, the government gained control of factories, stores, restaurants, and other small businesses.

When Mao initiated a program of collectivization—rural families sharing land and labor—people encouraged each other to join in the plan. Private property was abolished by the government. People who wanted to hold on to their property were criticized, jailed, or even executed. The government told citizens to work for the good of the society and not for personal gain.

At the end of the 1950s, when China had not become as rich and modern as Mao had hoped, he launched the One Hundred Flowers Campaign. In 1956 he asked people to give their views of the Communist Party and the central government—supposedly to help improve the party. Many spoke out, but Deng Xiaoping held back, unsure of Mao's next step. Critics claimed that the Communist Party was corrupt, medical research was outdated, and that China's teachers were unqualified. Intellectuals offered advice on how to reorganize and save China.

Then suddenly, Mao felt threatened by this criticism, and he reversed his plan. He launched a new campaign called antirightism. Mao and his supporters denounced anyone who had spoken openly against the Communist Party or the government. He gave Deng Xiaoping the job of finding the critics, or the rightists. The new campaign frightened people, and they became silent and tense.

Deng went at his new task with a fury. He was sure of what Mao wanted, and he condemned anyone reported to be a rightist. He encouraged workers to report bosses, students to report teachers, children to report neighbors or parents. People could no longer speak freely.

More than one million people were labeled anti-rightist and antiparty. Most of them were intellectuals—students, professors, writers, entrepreneurs, or scientists. The majority of them were sent to labor camps in the distant countryside. The luckier ones were simply demoted in their jobs. Many of those sent away spent years doing outdoor farm labor while receiving near-starvation rations—sometimes water and one corn-mash bun per day.

Deng Xiaoping had done well for himself by correctly anticipating Mao's moves. In 1956 Mao rewarded Deng by appointing him general secretary of the newly established Secretariat, a central executive institution of the Communist government. Because of Mao's support, Deng was also elected to the Politburo Standing Committee, the top governmental committee. He was sixth in rank on the committee—alongside his respected colleague Zhou Enlai. According to some Chinese scholars, however, Deng was actually second in command after Mao. In just seven years, Deng had moved up as far as he could in Mao's official lineup. Staying there was a matter of accurate political judgment.

The next major social and economic movement in China was the Great Leap Forward of 1958. This, too, caused chaos, but Mao believed that to bring about revolutionary changes, you had to allow revolutionary disruption. He stated, "A revolution is not a dinner party, or writing an essay, or painting a picture, or doing embroidery; it cannot be so refined, so leisurely and gentle, so temperate, kind, courteous, restrained and magnanimous. A revolution is an insurrection, an act of violence by which one class overthrows another."

Zhou Enlai, left, *Mao Zedong,* second from left, *Zhu De,* fourth from left, *and Deng Xiaoping,* far right, *met with Chinese scientists in the 1950s to discuss ways to improve industrial output.*

The Great Leap Forward sent China into a state of despair. Mao wanted a faster-growing economy and increased production, so he set China on an impossible course to surpass Britain's rate of industry over the next seven years. Although this industrial growth demanded more money and technology than China had, and it seemed impossible to many of Mao's colleagues, nobody tried to stop him.

Mao chided those who showed no enthusiasm for his new program. Instead of pointing out the error of the plan, Mao's economic advisers let him follow a nonsensical course. Wanting to stay in good favor and perhaps hoping Mao could be correct, Deng Xiaoping supported the launch of the Great

Leap Forward. He even acted as Mao's spokesperson. Deng traveled with Mao on an inspection tour of rural communes. During this period, Mao recognized Deng's support. Later he claimed that Deng was highly intelligent and predicted a great future for him.

With the Great Leap Forward, families gave up homes to live communally and work day and night. Parents sent their children to commune nurseries. The populace was dedicated to following Mao's dream and increasing China's rate of industry. But no one had thought out a realistic agricultural or industrial plan.

Mao wanted huge crop yields. He set impossible goals of doubling crop production, but local officials promised him what he wanted. When too little grain was grown, people falsified reports for the government. Thus, after the central government took its percentage of grain for the state, local people were left with next to nothing to eat. They dug for roots to fill their bellies.

Because Mao wanted increased steel production, people built homemade refineries to produce steel in their communes. They used every piece of wood in sight—even coffins—to fuel fires. They gathered every metal tool, pot, pan, and medallion and melted them in their refineries. If anyone did not participate, he or she was accused of being rightist. Not wanting to be sent to a labor camp, people carried out whatever program Mao endorsed.

The small refineries produced only useless globs of metal. Upon Mao's urging, people had destroyed forests and useful household items to make junk. At the same time, they had ignored their farming while feeding the refineries. Crops died from the lack of care.

Mao had also told the country to get rid of pests. People

killed insects furiously. They also killed pesky sparrows. They gathered thousands of the dead birds and piled them up for display. They applauded their collective work. They were proud to have participated in Mao's national campaign. But with all the sparrows gone, insects had no enemy. The insect population increased. Swarms of insects devoured the meager crops that grew.

Agricultural specialists may have understood the impending disaster that would afflict China. Most likely they kept silent instead of risking punishment. Mao's Great Leap Forward caused crops to fail. In fact, agricultural yields were

During the Great Leap Forward, Chinese peasants dug model fields that were supposed to produce very high yields.

From left: *Zhou Enlai, Chen Yun, Liu Shaoqi, Mao Zedong, Deng Xiaoping, and Peng Zhen discussed new plans for China at a conference of the Chinese Communist Party's Central Committee in 1962.*

so low that twenty million people starved to death between 1959 and 1961. Instead of going forward, China's industrial production declined, and the country experienced a severe economic depression.

Deng Xiaoping was one of the top political officials who kept silent despite misgivings about Mao's economic failure. Finally, he and a few colleagues felt responsible for finding an economic solution that would not cause Mao any humiliation. Deng was faced with a struggle.

Deng, foreground, *accompanied by Liu Shaoqi,* left, *Zhou Enlai,* second from left, *and Peng Zhen,* in white, *visited the Soviet Union, as a delegate to the Soviet-Chinese Ideology Talks in Moscow in the early 1960s.*

SIX

THE CULTURAL REVOLUTION

After the Great Leap Forward, many of China's officials criticized Mao's leadership, but they were unwilling to risk openly opposing him. Nobody wanted to anger Mao and face punishment for having incorrect political views. But which political views were correct? Mao had a habit of changing course whenever he felt he was losing power. The officials under Mao were unsure how to handle his radical decisions and actions. They needed a solution to China's economic crisis, and they had to find one that pleased Mao.

In addition to causing famine, Mao was also responsible for a split between China and the Soviet Union in 1963. The Soviets had helped China develop Communism. Many officials still wanted Soviet guidance and money for Chinese projects. But Mao had his own vision of Communist policy, outlined in a speech Deng gave in Moscow in July 1963. Deng was in the Soviet Union for two weeks of negotiations. The two Communist governments discussed the international Communist movement and the future of Communism. Some of Deng's statements—which reflected Mao's thoughts and beliefs—were uncompromising. He proposed that: (1) world war is inevitable as long as imperialism exists; (2) the only way to achieve socialism is through armed struggle, not through parliamentary elections; and (3) neither cooperation nor coexistence with any capitalist country can be allowed. After almost two weeks of arguing, the Soviets, who disagreed with these ideas, saw no way for constructive discussion. The two Communist parties broke off formal relations.

That same year, Mao recognized that the Great Leap Forward was a failure. He let others try to correct the agricultural and industrial disasters it had caused. In the forefront were Deng Xiaoping and a man name Liu Shaoqi. Liu had also studied in the Soviet Union in the 1920s, and he had worked in Yan'an as one of Mao's closest lieutenants. Deng and Liu worked together planning China's economic recovery.

Instead of carrying on with Mao's mass movements and hurried development, Deng and Liu slowed down economic development. They dismantled communes to restore farm production. They looked for practical solutions to create a more stable country. Deng worked by the motto of seeking truth from facts. He preferred cautious planning to upheaval and chaos.

In a 1962 speech to the Chinese Communist Youth League, Deng made a statement that became his most famous, even though he did not invent the coined phrase. He was talking about how to increase productivity. He believed that regional governments should develop whatever method worked best for them and not worry about continuing past policies if they did not help recovery. He quoted a Chinese proverb, the wording of which was later changed and preserved ("yellow" was changed to "white") as a famous Deng saying: "It does not matter if it is a yellow cat or a black cat, as long as it catches mice."

Deng and Liu, who were flexible and practical about economic theory, saw China recovering as they had hoped. Mao, however, worried that Chinese people were returning to middle-class living and thinking. He wanted to consolidate working-class power again, as he had done in the civil war against the Nationalists and in the Great Leap Forward. Mao wanted more class struggle—not a return to a country of rich professionals and poor workers and peasants.

For a few years, Mao let Deng and Liu run the country's economic recovery. They carried out reform policies without consulting Mao about each decision. This annoyed Mao, but he grumbled without interfering. "Deng is a deaf mute," Mao said, "but whenever he was at a conference, he always chose to sit in a spot far from me. He respected me but kept away from me, treating me like a dead ancestor."

Actually, by this point, Deng had become hard of hearing and he wore hearing aids. Because of this, Mao expected Deng to sit close to him at meetings to hear Mao's words. However, Deng believed that Mao had stopped listening to

Liu Shaoqi (right) *worked with Deng to solve problems caused by the Great Leap Forward.*

others and was no longer acting in the best interests of China. Deng was losing respect for his mentor. Deng thought Communism was supposed to be government by committee. He thought Mao was acting like an emperor.

Deng and Liu were not Mao's only critics. Other members of the central government and many intellectuals began to openly jab at Mao's policies of the 1950s and early 1960s. Mao's third wife, Jiang Qing, a former actress, supported her husband, but few people liked her. She had a reputation of being an ambitious schemer, but Mao promised that she would stay out of politics.

Jiang Qing stayed primarily behind the scenes until Mao began consulting her on political matters in the early 1960s. Little by little, she gained power. By 1963 she had become an influential person, especially in China's cultural scene. She censored many plays that did not meet her standards for correct revolutionary philosophy. By using Mao's statements against bourgeois and counterrevolutionary thinking, Jiang Qing manipulated artists she did not like. She controlled the selection of plays and cast members for national performances.

As Deng, Liu, and other Communist officials gained more power, Mao felt threatened. Although he had chosen to step aside politically, he did not want to give up his seat as China's paramount leader. He sometimes complained about Deng, Liu, and Zhou Enlai to his wife. Although Jiang Qing and Mao also had their own private troubles that led to their estrangement, in public Jiang Qing used Mao's power as her own. Many people have said that she was waiting for Mao's death so that she could take control of China. She viewed Deng and Liu as a threat to her as much as to Mao. Deng considered her intensely evil.

The more the government steered away from Mao's plan

of social upheaval, the angrier he became. With encouragement from Jiang Qing, Mao began to take power again. He said that if he were ousted, he would go into the countryside, unite his army, and overthrow the government. By 1965 Mao doubted the loyalty of his officials and accused Deng and Liu of trying to keep him out of meetings and block him from speaking. The Beijing government was in a political tangle, and the military was also reshuffling leadership.

In November 1965, Deng took his family on an inspection tour of his former region in southwestern China. Deng wanted to avoid political infighting in the central government. As always, Deng was watching Mao's behavior and trying to avoid serious conflict. In Chongqing, Deng met an appreciative welcoming committee. The party secretary of the southwestern region held a banquet in Deng's honor. After the dinner party, the guests played bridge until dawn. Deng said he played to relax his mind and forget Beijing politics.

When Deng and his family returned to Beijing, the political turmoil had grown worse. Confusion in Beijing's leadership was mirrored by confusion among the people. Students began denouncing certain local party leaders and university professors. They put up signs attacking individuals for middle-class thinking. These defiant acts ignited unrest on campuses and grew into a mass movement against party leaders who strayed from Mao's doctrines.

Deng and Liu hoped to quiet the students, but Mao wanted to use the unrest to launch a revolution. Deng and Liu sent work teams to the universities to support the students while protecting the teachers and the administration. The work teams found their task impossible. They could not keep the students from demonstrating in the streets and starting a national revolution. Unlike Deng and Liu, Mao was pleased

Mao's wife, Jiang Qing, left, and Zhou Enlai, second from right, spoke at a massive Communist rally in Beijing in 1966, at the start of the Cultural Revolution.

with this chaos and encouraged it. With such popular support, Mao was ready to show his strength once again.

On July 16, 1966, Mao pulled a media stunt. Mao, at age seventy-three, insisted on swimming down the Yangtze River, even though he knew of the dangerous conditions of the water. Surrounded by guards, Mao jumped into the water. The media publicized his act. The photos were meant to prove that Mao was invincible and to signal his return to power. The Cultural Revolution, as the next ten years have been called, was building momentum.

While Deng Xiaoping searched for a moderate position, Mao stirred up revolutionary fever. Mao demanded that Liu and Deng dissolve the work teams. He threatened the government, warning, "If you don't make revolution, the revolution will be directed against you."

On August 1, 1966, Mao wrote a letter to a young student who had organized a group of prorevolutionary youths called the Red Guards. Mao told this student that rebellion was justified. That statement, published in many school newspapers, inspired students to join the Red Guards, a semimilitary organization. Those who did not were considered counter-revolutionary and anti-Mao. Red Guards marched in the streets and attacked Communist Party leaders and their headquarters. Out with corruption, they declared. Destroy China's enemies of socialism. Eliminate the Four Olds—old thought, old culture, old customs, and old habits.

Nobody felt safe. The Red Guards invaded homes throughout China to search for evidence of corruption and disloyalty to the social revolution. If the Guards saw fancy furniture, they smashed it. They tore old photos apart. Luxuries could cost a family its survival. They destroyed any memento that glorified the past and its owners along with it.

The Red Guards also attacked authority figures such as teachers, parents, and workplace managers. Children accused their own mothers and fathers. Neighbors accused neighbors. And the Red Guards themselves splintered into different factions, often battling each other. In street fighting alone, tens of thousands of citizens died.

The economy and social services of China collapsed. Factories failed, transportation was interrupted, schools became fighting grounds or shut down completely. New music, art, theater, and literature replaced traditional works. Art now portrayed the hard work and dedication of China's working class.

In August 1966, Liu Shaoqi and Deng Xiaoping found themselves in political trouble. As was his habit, Deng moved away from dangerous politics—in this case Liu's politics—and sided more closely with Mao. Because Deng and Liu had sent out work teams to quiet the revolution, they now had to confess their errors.

In a governmental meeting with Mao and others, both men gave confessions. Deng's words were much more apologetic than Liu's. Deng stated that he was a petty, middle-class intellectual who had interfered with Mao's socialist education movement. He said he needed to abandon his old way of thinking and correct his errors so that he could later do something valuable for the party and for the people.

After Deng spoke, Mao stood up to make his views clear. He said that Deng and Liu were not the only officials in error. However, Mao was displeased with the way Deng and Liu had abused their leadership roles and left Mao out of their

During the Cultural Revolution, students called Red Guards showed loyalty to their leader Mao Zedong, shown on a poster, *at demonstrations across China.*

Many Chinese were persecuted both publicly and privately during the Cultural Revolution. These Red Guards force some citizens to stand on trucks and wear dunce caps as punishment for being leaders of so-called "anti-revolutionary groups" in Beijing.

decision-making. He also said that the men should be given a chance to show their reform, but this chance was never given.

Mao's wife, Jiang Qing, and three prorevolution comrades (later called the Gang of Four) made sure that Deng and Liu were punished. She encouraged public anti-Deng and anti-Liu campaigns. Jiang Qing herself wrote an article listing Deng's crimes of treating Mao with contempt, opposing the reform of education and the arts, undoing the collectivization of agriculture, and practicing bourgeois dictatorship.

Jiang Qing encouraged the Red Guards to write articles that criticized Deng and Liu and to demonstrate against them in the streets. Red Guards eventually raided Liu's house and humiliated Liu and his wife. Then they forced the couple to criticize themselves publicly and jailed Liu while expelling him from the Communist Party. Just over one year later, Liu contracted pneumonia in jail. Mao denied Liu medical care, and the former Communist lieutenant died alone.

The Red Guards also came to Deng Xiaoping's home. Deng was stripped of his government titles but was allowed to keep his party membership. During one session, Red Guards made Deng kneel on the floor with his arms stretched out behind him and over his head. Deng's family watched as Red Guards ordered Deng to confess his capitalist thinking. Deng feared that Red Guards would kill him and his family. Later Deng said that even though Mao supported the Red Guards attack, he had saved Deng from imprisonment or death. Deng believed that Jiang Qing would have killed him if Mao had not been in power.

However, Deng's older son, Deng Pufang, did not escape tragedy. When Red Guards came after him at Beijing University, he either fell, threw himself, or was pushed out of a window. Still alive on the concrete below, Deng Pufang was rushed to the university hospital. The hospital staff denied Deng Pufang admission because he was the son of a "capitalist." By the time the young man reached another clinic, he was paralyzed from the waist down.

In October 1969, Mao sent Deng, Deng's wife, and his stepmother to Nanchang in the Jiangxi Province. There the family lived in two downstairs rooms of a four-room building. The People's Liberation Army soldiers who guarded the family slept in two upstairs rooms. Guards brought Deng and his wife food and fuel, but the couple had to fend for themselves if they needed anything else.

Deng and his wife worked in a tractor repair shop in the mornings—he as a machine operator and she as a cleaning woman—and often gardened in the afternoons. Deng's stepmother, who stayed in the house, did much of the housework and cooking. When not at work, Deng chopped wood, broke up coal, and sometimes pitched in on the indoor chores. In his spare time, he paced in the little courtyard in front of the house and planned a return to Beijing.

In the summer of 1971, Mao must have relaxed Deng's house arrest, because the family was allowed to take over both floors of the home, and the armed soldiers were replaced by unarmed guards. Deng's oldest son, Deng Pufang, was then allowed to go to Nanchang to live with his parents. Deng, who had not seen his son since the accident, was horrified by his paralysis. Deng spent much time bathing and caring for Deng Pufang, trying to lift his son's spirits during that depressing period. In the same season, Deng Rong, Deng's youngest daughter, and Deng Zhifang, his second son, also spent time with their parents.

At the end of 1971, China's central government suffered more significant changes. Mao lost patience with his designated successor, a man named Lin Biao, and with Chen Boda,

Deng Pufang, Deng Xiaoping's oldest son, was permanently injured during the Cultural Revolution when he fell, jumped, or was pushed out of a window at Beijing University.

one of the Gang of Four. Mao took measures to remove Lin from office, and then Lin Biao took countermeasures. Lin asked his son, a staff officer in the air force, to plan the assassination of Mao, but Mao discovered the murder plot. On September 13, 1971, Lin Biao, his wife, and his son died in a plane crash in the desert of Outer Mongolia. The leadership of China was once again in flux.

When Deng Xiaoping heard the latest political news from Beijing in November 1971, he wrote to Mao asking to be allowed back to the city and reassigned work. In Deng's letter, he declared that he supported the Cultural Revolution for its uncovering of Lin Biao's true murderous nature. Deng wrote of his political conflicts with Lin Biao and of his own political reform. Deng said he was overjoyed by Mao's victory against the treacherous Lin Biao. Deng knew just what to write to persuade Mao to reconsider him for a government position. Deng's first letter went unanswered, so he wrote a second on August 3, 1972. Deng wrote apologetic words:

> As the Chairman knows, Lin Biao and Chen Boda hated me and would rather have put me to death. I can hardly imagine what might have happened to me but for the Chairman's protection . . . It has been almost six years since I have been out of work and out of society. I have always been looking forward to an opportunity to return to the Chairman's revolutionary line. Being sixty-eight years old and still in decent health, I may still work seven or eight more years for the party and for the people, redeeming some small part of my previous blunders.

After receiving the second letter, Mao softened. He decided that China could use an experienced man like Deng Xiaoping in the government. Although he had not forgotten Deng's errors, Mao applauded Deng's past military successes and his anti-Soviet activities. Zhou Enlai also supported Deng's return.

Finally in February 1973, Deng and his family left Jiangxi by train for Beijing. They moved into a house in the northeastern quarter of the city and waited for word of Deng's new job. Members of the Communist Party Center debated Deng's next assignment. Some wanted to offer him only a research position, but Mao made the final decision. Deng was appointed as a vice premier. He went to work again under his old comrade Zhou Enlai, who was in charge of the politburo's routine affairs.The politburo was the political unit of the Communist Party, and all important decisions had to get the approval of its members. Deng had tactfully found his way back into the government.

In 1974 Deng, right, chatted with U.S. Secretary of State Henry Kissinger, left, at a dinner in New York City. At the time, Deng was the highest-ranking official of the People's Republic of China to ever visit the United States.

SEVEN

POLITICAL DEATH AND REBIRTH

In 1973 the Chinese political scene that Deng rejoined was again insecure and full of dispute in the highest ranks. Jiang Qing and her Gang of Four still actively opposed Deng. But this time, Deng rallied his own colleagues. He understood that although he could not rely on Mao, he did have to respect and please him. Mao had dismissed Deng before, and he could do so again.

Deng also knew that he would have to take small steps in his new political career and pay close attention to Mao's moods and governmental decisions. Deng's toughest problems were Mao's unpredictability and Jiang Qing's growing power. As long as Mao did not stop her, Madame Mao, as she was also called, could bring down whomever she disliked. And she disliked both Zhou Enlai and Deng Xiaoping. Deng wanted to regain power, but he was very sly and patient in doing so. He did what he could to please Mao, and then he watched the others in power.

In his first year back, Deng had little government responsibility. In July 1952, when Mao first summoned Deng to Beijing, Mao was watching him, slowly handing him more and more authority. When Deng made his first public reappearance on April 12, 1973, in the Great Hall of the People, the guests were surprised to see this familiar little man stride into the crowd. They gave him smiles and applause. Zhou Enlai then introduced Deng as the deputy premier to guest Prince Sihanouk, former head of Cambodia.

In 1973 Deng became China's official greeter of foreign visitors. He appeared publicly on about one hundred occasions, receiving foreign visitors, attending official holiday celebrations, offering greetings at conferences, and going to state funerals. He worked with seriousness and diplomacy.

In August 1973, Deng was allowed to renew his membership on the Party Central Committee, and he waited patiently to see how Mao would use him. In December Mao made public statements about Deng's usefulness and talents. Mao claimed that Deng is "pretty resolute in tackling problems" and is a man of "softness melded with toughness." Finally, Mao proposed that Deng be accepted as a full member of the politburo and of the Central Military Council. Whatever Mao wanted, Mao achieved. Deng was promoted again.

During this period, Mao was becoming frustrated by Zhou Enlai's actions in the government. Zhou had been diagnosed with stomach cancer in 1972, and neither his health nor his moderate political decisions helped him win Mao's favor. Mao became obsessed with finding the right successor for the role of chairman. Zhou was no longer a good choice. Deng Xiaoping became one of the candidates.

In April 1974, Deng was offered the opportunity to represent China as a delegate to a special session of the United Nations General Assembly in New York City. Jiang Qing had been opposed to Mao's choice of Deng, but Mao ordered her not to oppose his decisions. Foreign affairs officials and international relations scholars in China wrote Deng's speech. All Deng had to do was read it clearly and confidently, which he did. Deng earned a great deal of respect and publicity outside of China, and Mao was very pleased with his performance. Before leaving New York, Deng toured the city and learned just what a modern city looked like. Upon Deng's return to Beijing, Zhou Enlai and many senior party, government, and military officials welcomed him at the airport. Although Mao was not there, he later rewarded Deng with more governmental promotions.

The more authority Deng was given, the more he had to tangle with Jiang Qing and her gang. At a politburo meeting on October 17, 1974, Deng and Jiang argued openly. Disliking such conflict, Deng finally stood up and walked out of the conference hall.

In January 1975, at the age of seventy, Deng attended the Fourth People's Congress of the Communist Party. Mao had again proposed Deng for several positions, and the Congress members elected Deng to each of these. Again, Mao controlled party elections. Deng became vice chairman of the Military Council, vice chairman of the Central Committee, vice premier of the State Administrative Council, and chief of staff of the People's Liberation Army. This move gave Deng great power over Jiang Qing and her gang. They, in turn, wanted revenge.

In his new positions, Deng immediately set out to correct organizational problems in the government. He also developed a firm economic strategy for China. Deng promoted a concept called the Four Modernizations—modernization in agriculture, industry, national defense, and science and technology. He spoke to industrial leaders, transportation specialists, scientists, and the Military Council to propose

In 1975 U.S. Secretary of State Henry Kissinger, second from left, *President Gerald Ford,* third from left, *then-ambassador to Beijing George Bush,* fourth from left, *joked with Deng Xiaoping,* second from right, *and other Chinese officials at an international economic summit meeting in Beijing.*

methods for improving efficiency and ending corruption. Deng believed that economic production was much more important for China than political revolution. Statistics proved that Deng was effective. In 1975 China's economy grew 11.9 percent, a great increase over the 1974 rate of 1.4 percent.

What Deng did not do in 1975 was prepare and spread Communist propaganda. This was the job of Jiang Qing. Deng mocked Jiang's work when he was in private, but he supported it publicly because Mao approved of it. Deng did whatever he thought best for China, unless his plans went against Mao's special interests. Keeping Mao's favor was crucial.

Although Deng seemed to be working with Mao's constant approval, the political atmosphere was unclear. Before long, Mao, whose health was failing rapidly, became dissatisfied with Deng again. Deng's opponents—like Jiang Qing—criticized Deng. Mao felt that Deng had forgotten about class struggle, a concept that Mao still endorsed firmly. The Gang of Four sensed Mao's changing opinion of Deng, and they planned to topple Deng for good. In the meantime, Mao had to choose his successor, and Deng had several marks against him. Before Mao made his decision, he had to face another political shift. Zhou Enlai, the acting premier, died on January 8, 1976. The public thought Mao would visit Zhou at his bedside. Zhou had been Mao's loyal sidekick, but in the end Mao totally ignored him. The people were shocked.

Zhou was an old revolutionary whom the people had loved. Having survived all the turbulence since the 1920s, Zhou had become a popular Chinese hero. In Tiananmen Square, the public openly mourned Zhou's death and expressed their loathing of the manipulative Gang of Four that had worked against Zhou. Deng Xiaoping had visited Zhou in the hospital days before he died, and he gave the formal address to the Central Committee for Zhou's funeral service.

As much as Jiang Qing wanted an official position of authority, Mao knew he could not choose his wife to replace Zhou Enlai as premier. However, Deng was no longer a wise choice because his political moves again seemed capitalist and counterrevolutionary. Mao believed in his Cultural Revolution, and Deng made the mistake of ignoring it. In a surprising move, Mao chose a little-known man named Hua Guofeng as acting premier. Hua had been a party secretary from Mao's native province and was thought to be likable and honest. The radicals in the government were disappointed by Mao's choice.

In March 1976, the politburo held several conferences to criticize Deng's leadership. Mao and Hua believed that Deng had made mistakes but was still worthy of another chance. The radicals openly demanded Deng's swift removal, but Deng maintained silence in the face of their criticism.

Some college students attended one politburo conference as representatives of the revolutionary masses. When the students criticized Deng's rightist activities, Deng stood up and walked out. He was quoted as having said, "I am a deaf old man, and I could not hear what you folks were yelling about."

In the same month, a public event turned into a major political upheaval that changed Deng's life again. In late March, some schoolchildren left a bouquet of pink roses on the marble pedestal of the People's Heroes Monument in Tiananmen Square. They left the flowers in honor of Zhou Enlai. By early April, more mourners had placed funeral wreaths upon the monument in honor of Zhou. Then people hung banners saying that the people missed Premier Zhou and that Premier Zhou was immortal. On April 4, 1976, almost two million people visited the monument.

The Beijing government was angered by the mass gathering and the political messages on the monument. The politburo gave the police permission to remove all the wreaths during the night of April 4. The next day, about one million people came back to the square demanding the return of their wreaths. Conflicts between the police and the mourners lasted well into the night. Then about ten thousand militiamen arrived and brutally beat hundreds of demonstrators.

The politburo called an emergency meeting, but Hua Guofeng was unsure what to do. The radicals, however, found their moment to strike. They declared that Deng Xiaoping had been the instigator of the riot and should be immediately removed from office. This time, Mao sided with the radicals and demoted Deng again. As he had done in 1967, Mao allowed Deng to keep his party membership.

Deng made no public confession of his errors this time. He would not humiliate himself in front of Jiang Qing. He simply submitted a paper of self-criticism to Mao and to the politburo and watched as Beijing politics unraveled.

Mao was close to death. While he was removing Deng from office, Mao formally appointed Hua first vice chairman of the Party Center, making Hua the person who would replace Chairman Mao when he died. This move thwarted the radicals who wanted one of their own to take Mao's place.

On September 9, 1976, Chairman Mao Zedong died. The country was stunned and anxious about the future. Young people knew Mao as the symbol of the People's Republic of China. Older military people thought of him as their great revolutionary leader. Some Chinese were in awe of Chairman Mao, but others were critical of his political and economic blunders. The people knew Mao, but they did not know Hua Guofeng. They wondered how their country would change.

Hua Guofeng

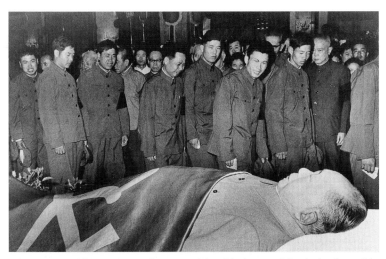

Throngs of Chinese people passed by Chairman Mao's body at his funeral in 1976. They were uncertain about the future of the People's Republic of China without their leader.

Although Mao had chosen Hua Guofeng to succeed him, Jiang and her gang had no intention of letting Hua take over as chairman. Hua knew of the gang's plotting, and he planned his own political move. He secretly called a politburo meeting on October 5 to discuss the transfer of governmental power. The next day, Hua had the Gang of Four arrested, an event that caused citizens to come out and cheer in the streets. (They would not be tried until 1980.)

After Deng's removal from office, he either confined himself, or was confined, to his Beijing home. Whether or not he and his family were guarded against their will is unclear. Deng lived privately with his family and learned what he could about the political changes going on.

As soon as Deng heard that the Gang of Four had been arrested, he stepped back into the political arena. He made offers of advice to Hua Guofeng and fought artfully for acceptance back into the Central Committee. In a letter he wrote to Hua on October 10, 1975, Deng flattered Hua in the same way he had flattered Mao in his letters of 1972.

Deng wrote that Hua was the most appropriate successor to Chairman Mao. He also wrote that, because Hua was young, he could lead China for the next fifteen or twenty years. Deng made these statements simply to win Hua's favor. He did not mean what he wrote, just as he had not meant what he wrote to Mao in 1972 or what he wrote in his many confessions. Deng was finally allowed to return to the movement—this time to make major strides toward improving China's future.

Deng quickly gained political support from his former colleagues. He soon became more powerful than the less experienced Hua Guofeng. In July 1977, at the Tenth Party Congress held in Beijing, the Congress members voted to reinstate all of Deng's former titles. For a while, Deng shared top power with Hua Guofeng, but this arrangement soon faltered. Hua was not dynamic as chairman. He kept his title but lost his authority to Deng Xiaoping.

In the fall of 1978, a new form of public protest arose in China. Young workers called for more social and political freedom, and people gathered in the streets to voice their opinions about China's government. Intellectuals began putting up political posters on a long wall near a busy Beijing intersection. This wall soon came to be known as Democracy Wall. In their posters, people criticized Mao and the Gang of Four, while they praised Zhou Enlai and Deng Xiaoping. The mood of the country was swinging away from leftist revolution and toward democratic freedom.

Deng Xiaoping supported the Democracy Wall for weeks. The sentiments that were posted seemed to be in his favor. Throughout the Cultural Revolution, people had concealed their feelings and political views for fear of being attacked by the Red Guards. Afterward, they could openly discuss politics, and they took joy in doing so. Soon larger crowds, interested in debating political theories, gathered around the wall. The participants hoped that Deng would encourage political debate as he had encouraged modern economic planning.

Political liberalization, however, was not Deng's intention. He was still a staunch Communist. That meant that the masses had to follow party politics and not hope for a capitalist system that allowed freedom of speech and assembly. Eventually, the Democracy Wall crowds grew too big and the posters became critical of Deng's politics. Deng ordered the police to remove the posters and close off entrance to the Democracy Wall intersection.

Although Deng was a Communist, he wanted to replace

Deng demanded that posters on the Democracy Wall in Beijing be removed after they began to show criticism of his policies.

the radical ideology of the Cultural Revolution with new ideology for an economically sound China. He went back to the program of Four Modernizations and said nothing about revolution or class struggle. Deng planned rapid educational and technological advances, and he knew how to achieve them. One of his methods was to encourage international relations, especially with the United States. He wanted financial assistance from the West for China's economic, educational, and industrial modernization.

In January 1979, the United States and China diplomatically recognized each other. Deng returned to the United States one month later to meet President Jimmy Carter and to discuss joint business ventures between the two countries. Carter happily received Deng and his wife, and Deng's U.S. tour was a great success. China was proud to see its leader meeting with President Carter. American politicians and business leaders were enthusiastic about keeping an open policy between China and the United States. This policy quickly brought Western books, ideas, and tourists to China.

During the 1980s, Deng Xiaoping was the most powerful leader in China. His approval was necessary for all major political decisions. Deng was also popular overseas for opening China to international business. Deng remained faithful to Communist beliefs, but he eventually loosened many social constraints on the people. Until his time, people were assigned jobs by the state and lived wherever the state dictated. People also had little freedom in what they studied in school or how they could use their talents.

Deng created new laws that allowed people to go to school for a career of their own choosing, start their own businesses, and choose their own marriage partners and homes. He was also willing to try new ventures. He even allowed his

Deng, left foreground, *and Hua Guofeng,* right, with shovel, waving, *gave appearances of cooperation by joining Chinese Communist Party leaders in planting trees near Beijing on China's national tree-planting day. In reality, Deng had full control of China.*

son Deng Pufang to promote rock bands that had formerly been banned by conservative hard-liners. One China expert wrote, "Deng's idea in general was this: Float it. Try something. If it works, great. If it doesn't work, clamp it down."

Although Deng was much more liberal than his Communist predecessors, he still kept firm control through the authority of the Communist Party. Chinese people still lived in fear of government interference in their personal lives, and corruption in the party and in local governments was rampant. Ordinary citizens often went to jail for not paying a bribe to a police chief or for opposing a local official.

One middle-aged woman in Beijing, nervous and wary, wrote in poor English about her miserable life controlled by Chinese authorities. In 1986 she was brave enough to hand her writings to two female American tourists outside a Beijing museum. She wanted them to tell foreign radio and television stations about real life in China. Her letter, addressed hurriedly "please here letter—Dear Mr and Lady—Thank you!" gives a sorry picture of corruption:

> Dear Mr and Lady—
> Beijing policeman kill my son. Matter is this: I was worker. Boss dismiss me work. Because one policeman wanted to marry with me. He had four son. He old 20 years than I. I didn't. After I marry with a man in the army. Policemaster with boss dismiss me work. My husband again marry. My family only I and my son. I and my son beg meal 9 years . . . My tears and my son's tears are rivers!!!
> Good man enter prison. Bad man is official . . . Policeman kill man, no matter. Policeman eat meat people's. Policeman drink people's blood . . . I with men prepare march-rally in Beijing in May 6th 1986 year . . . I beg Mr. that my matter put newspaper on the world. Honest Mr. and Lady, save poor me and poor my son. We'll no forget one's life!

In 1980 the Gang of Four and other criminals stood trial for treason and other crimes committed during the Cultural Revolution. The gang included Yao Wenyuan (far left), Zhang Chunqiao (second from left), Jiang Qing (far right), and Wang Hongwen (not pictured). With the gang's public humiliation, Deng further consolidated his political authority.

Deng with his wife Zhou Lin in the 1980s

The Chinese government remained full of contradictions. For example, state-controlled television publicized dozens of rags-to-riches stories of ordinary Chinese people. What the government did not publicize was the corruption and the underhanded dealings behind those rags-to-riches stories. Critics inside and outside China began to ask, Could China become capitalist in its economy without becoming democratic in its politics? Deng answered yes.

China saw a growing chasm between its elderly Communist Party leaders like Deng Xiaoping and its modern-day reformers. Conservative Communists wanted China to hold on to its tested social principles. Reformers wanted to move China toward democracy.

One reformer in the government and the Chinese Communist Party, Hu Yaobang, became outspoken and liberal in his new ideas for China. At first he was supported and groomed by Deng Xiaoping. When hard-liners became angry about the "spiritual pollution" in China, Hu spoke back. He announced that the only spiritual pollution in China occurred when someone tried to destroy the will of the people. At one time, people hoped Hu would take over after Deng died.

In the late 1980s, Deng encouraged technological and scientific advancement and open business practices. Deng traveled throughout China and met with scientists and technology experts to discuss China's future.

EIGHT

TUMULTUOUS CLIMATE

By 1989 China was in an unsettling period of transition. The economic and technological changes that Deng had ignited were unfamiliar to millions of Chinese who had lived under tight Communist control. Having had little personal choice in employment, housing, family finance, or education, many people were unsure how to make changes. Some Chinese grabbed for the chance to start a private business, while many others were afraid to let go of their secure state-controlled jobs. Laws were not yet firmly established to keep new businesses ethical and fair. The absence of laws led to confusion, corruption, poor business ethics, and a growing gap between the rich and the poor, between the powerful and the vulnerable.

Another complication in China's modernization was citizen misunderstanding about what could change and what could not. People who believed that economic freedom also meant freedom of speech and assembly were quickly disappointed. The Open-Door Policy on foreign imports and scholar exchange was meant to bring business to China and to train future technologists, economists, scientists, computer specialists, and entrepreneurs. The policy was not meant to uproot Communism. The Chinese Communist Party fought every threat to its system.

Prodemocracy Chinese—especially college-age students—were excited by news of the recent weakening of the Soviet Union's strict hold on the countries of Eastern Europe. They wanted to bring about social and political change in China. Students first demonstrated for changes such as better living conditions in their universities and for the removal of corrupt officials from office. Their demonstrations were often noisy, but their actions were usually not violent.

Deng Xiaoping and the collective leadership demanded that the students abide by the laws for public parades and strikes. Earlier, Deng had given his view of student demonstrations to a group of party veterans. He indicated his concerns for the future when he said, "Student uproar is not in itself a big deal, but its very nature suggests a big deal. . . . Since the Beijing government has announced regulations regarding parades and strikes, they have the status of law and must be implemented. . . . This is not just an issue in only one or two places, nor just an issue of only one or two years. It is a result of these several years' ambiguity and hesitation in fighting against bourgeois liberalization."

Deng was admitting that China's modernization and reform had brought about confusion. Instead of addressing the confusion, however, he limited public demonstrations. He was going to promote reform and economic liberalization, but he would not allow any challenge to the political system.

One party member who criticized Deng's policy and was stripped of party membership and his academic positions was Fang Lizhi, an astrophysicist. He wrote, "There's no denying that China's reforms are in big trouble. Modernization and democratization have come to a halt, unable to move forward even though the road back is cut off. All around us, societies of similar racial and cultural background are racing to join the ranks of the developed nations, while on the Chinese mainland time passes with little progress to report."

The year 1989 marked the anniversaries of several historical movements: the fortieth anniversary of the People's Republic of China (October 1, 1949), the seventieth anniversary of the May Fourth Movement in China (1919), and the two hundredth anniversary of the French Revolution (July 14, 1789), which marked the French people's overthrow of a repressive monarchy. In 1989 many Chinese citizens and Western friends hoped for a major change in China's government—toward democracy.

Encouraged by all these anniversaries, bold intellectuals approached China's leaders to ask for change. Fang Lizhi wrote Deng Xiaoping a letter on January 6, 1989:

> Chairman Deng Xiaoping
> This year is the fortieth anniversary of the founding of the People's Republic of China, and the seventieth anniversary of the May Fourth Movement . . . I would like to offer my sincere suggestion that on the occasion of these two anniversaries, a nationwide amnesty be declared, especially including the release of political prisoners such as Wei Jingsheng [founder of the Democracy Wall movement] . . . .

Although his letter was endorsed by ninety scholars in China and abroad, Fang Lizhi received no response from Deng Xiaoping. And Wei Jingsheng was not let out of prison. Reports from inside the government stated that Deng Xiaoping was infuriated by the letter. Other democracy supporters wrote letters to Chinese government leaders. Their letters were also unanswered.

The government faced trouble within its own ranks. Some leaders, such as Hu Yaobang, who had lost his leadership post in 1986, tolerated student demonstrations and looked for ways to speed up China's modernization. Others saw this period as a chance to wipe out the democracy movement for good. Because of his liberal views, Hu was forced to resign his position as secretary-general of the Chinese Communist Party. Deng stood between the two sides of the political debate. Modernization was important to him as long as it could be controlled by a stable Communist government.

In February 1989, Deng Xiaoping met with George Bush, then president of the United States. Bush unsuccessfully tried to bring Fang Lizhi to a party for Deng Xiaoping at the American Embassy, but Chinese police prevented Fang Lizhi from even getting near the embassy. When Bush raised the issue of political prisoners with Deng, the Chinese leader explained that China had many people, each with his or her own opinion. If China let everyone protest, the country would face protest 365 days of the year. If that were the case, how could China get on with modernization? Human rights were less important to Deng than maintaining a stable nation.

On April 15, 1989, Hu Yaobang died after suffering a heart attack during a politburo meeting. He had been arguing heatedly with conservatives in the meeting. For many Chinese, Hu had been a symbol of freedom and liberal politics, and they wanted to mourn his death openly, as they had mourned for Zhou. A few thousand students from Beijing University and the People's University wanted to show their respect to Hu by demonstrating in Tiananmen Square and calling for Hu's good reputation to be reestablished.

On Sunday and Monday, April 16 and 17, students put up a few memorial wreaths for Hu Yaobang in Tiananmen

In 1989 Deng, left, *met with President George Bush,* center, *and his wife, Barbara Bush,* right, *in Beijing.*

Square. They made speeches to the gathering people, and they hung a banner that read, "The Soul of China," which referred to Hu Yaobang.

By Monday afternoon, crowds poured into the square and added more wreaths and white paper flowers used for mourning in China. A giant portrait of Hu was mounted on the Monument to the People's Heroes. A few students stood out as leaders—Wang Dan, Chai Ling, Li Lu, Wu-er Kaixi, Shen Tong, and Wang Chaohua—but the spontaneous gathering was not, at that time, an organized demonstration.

In the next few days, people put up posters stating "the wrong man had died" and "a good man has died, but many bad ones are still living." They shouted for democracy and freedom. Armed policemen patrolled the area and gave reports of the scene through walkie-talkies to the central government. Although police had clashed with students in a couple of violent incidents, more and more people came to Tiananmen Square and packed the central Beijing streets.

On April 22, three students took another step to get the attention of China's leaders. They climbed the steps of the Great Hall of the People and knelt in front of the doors. They held high a scroll that listed their demands, and they offered it to the government. They said they wanted only an open dialogue with and respect from the government. Government leaders did not respond to the student representatives. For that reason, thousands of students decided to boycott classes and stay in Tiananmen Square until the government agreed to hold talks with them. Many students stayed on the square all day. Others decided to camp out for the night.

On April 26, 1989, Deng Xiaoping fueled the student demonstrations through an editorial in the *People's Daily* newspaper. In the article, Deng's appointed writers claimed that students intended to destroy party leadership and the Communist system through a planned conspiracy. The article, a warning to demonstrators, said the students wanted turmoil, and the government should move to stop it quickly. Deng was willing to take extreme action and did not worry about reproach from the Chinese people or from foreign governments. He said, "We do not fear spilling blood, and we do not fear the international reaction."

Students were stunned and offended by the April 26 article. They did not view their spontaneous mourning for Hu Yaobang or their wish for change as an organized attempt to topple the government. Students said they were very pro-China. They loved their homeland. They shouted slogans in the streets. Down with corrupt officials! Patriotism is not a crime! Continue the reforms!

One Chinese citizen remembers how she and her classmates felt as college students in 1989:

> At that time, most of us were eighteen to twenty years old. We had been depressed our whole lives. Our blood was hot, so the students in the whole country became a united force. We were not wrong to protest, to ask for freedom and a new life. It was my generation who tried to cry out.
>
> From birth to death we were slaves. We had no control over our lives. We were sent to get a slave's education in order to serve "Country and Communism." We were forced to learn by heart all the lies of the system. We were fooled as little kids and as college students. They [China's leaders] thought we were stupid. They did not realize we would have a voice. To them we were slaves. If we tried hard maybe we could become leaders of slaves like them, help them control and abuse other slaves. After graduation we could try hard, make good connections and get a nice job in the government. Then we could become slave masters. Most of us were from ordinary families without the right connections. We looked at the history of our country and saw decades and decades of corruption and unfair events. We were not going to be fooled again. We did not want to be slaves of the government. We wanted to have our voice, our equal rights, a better life and a better country. We loved the

country. We wanted it to be a better place. In China
we have a saying: It is always the people who suffer
no matter which side wins.

The next day, April 27, more than three hundred thousand people—students, parents, factory workers, shopkeepers, and onlookers—marched down Beijing streets and in
Tiananmen Square for fourteen hours. Although Deng had
called out troops to disperse the demonstrators, the police did
not want to use violence. People were exuberant. They
thought they had won a victory for democracy and that April
27 was the beginning of a new democratic revolution.

Demonstrations continued through the early part of May.
The students continued to try to achieve an open dialogue
with government leaders. The general secretary of the Communist Party, Zhao Ziyang, who had been in Korea when the
demonstrations started, spoke out in his May 4 anniversary
speech. He indicated a softening of the government position,
a willingness to meet and talk with students. His tone was
very different from Deng's in the April 26 editorial, and it
hinted at a split in the government.

After much argument among the poorly organized students, some decided to avoid a stalemate and return to
classes. They were tired of demonstrating. Student leader
Wang Dan told Canadian interviewers that he sought new
tactics:

> I think that the student movement should move on to
> a new stage. No more large-scale, intense street ac-
> tion, no more boycotting classes. Instead, we need
> down-to-earth work to build democracy on campus:
> the legalization of student organizations, independent
> student newspapers and radio stations. This work
> might not look all that grand or glamorous, but it's ex-
> tremely important.

Thousands of students gathered in 1989 on Beijing's large, open Tiananmen (or "Gate of Heavenly Peace") Square to protest the Chinese government's treatment of its citizens.

A few days later, Wang Dan and others decided to go on a hunger strike. Chai Ling, an emotional student leader, wanted to join the strike and gave a tearful, impassioned speech on May 12, proclaiming, "We are staging a hunger strike in order to reveal the true face of the government and the true face of the people. We want to see whether the

Chinese have any conscience, whether there is any hope for China."

About two hundred students decided to join the strike. They painted "starving for democracy" on black headbands, and on May 13 they stopped eating. The students had to get permission from their parents to die. In China, suicide is viewed as a severe disrespect of one's ancestors, and the hunger strike was a method of protest completely alien to China. This strike did bring a measure of compromise from the government. Officials agreed to talk to the students and broadcast the dialogue live on television.

However, the May 14 talks got off to a bitter start. Conservative premier Li Peng arrived late. Wu-er Kaixi asked Li Peng why he was late. Li Peng rambled, and Wu-er Kaixi interrupted him. Impatient, Wu-er Kaixi and the other student representatives did not want to listen to Li Peng's pleasantries. Some clear points were made on both sides. But then some students from the streets, who mistakenly thought the conversation was not being broadcast, disrupted the meeting. Talks broke down before real agreements had been made, and Wu-er Kaixi collapsed during the televised talks.

The hunger strike continued. Chai Ling, who worried that the government did not care if the students starved to death, threatened that she and others might set themselves on fire to get more attention.

By the third day of the hunger strike, the situation in Beijing was grim. Deng Xiaoping was agitated by the demonstrations at a time when he sought world approval for the modernization of China. He was about to meet with Soviet president Mikhail Gorbachev, the first Soviet leader to visit China in thirty years. In front of media cameras, Deng's face was tight and cheerless.

Gorbachev arrived on May 15, with three thousand journalists who were paying close attention to his meeting with Deng. Because of the crowd of demonstrators in Tiananmen Square, Gorbachev's formal greeting and several scheduled events had to be relocated or canceled. Gorbachev observed the uncontrolled crowds in the square, which further annoyed Deng. In Deng Xiaoping's mind, the students had earned several more strikes against them for interrupting international diplomatic plans.

Instead of focusing on the Sino-Soviet summit meeting, the international journalists quickly became more interested in the Chinese students' hunger strike. Ambulances zoomed in and out of the square picking up ailing students who had collapsed from their fast. Student leaders shouting noisy demands were televised internationally. And Deng Xiaoping, who had wanted journalistic attention on his historic meeting with Gorbachev, was left in the shadows of the media.

The standoff in the square continued throughout the latter part of May. Some art students at the Central Academy of Fine Arts built a giant statue that resembled the Statue of Liberty, and they called it the "Goddess of Democracy." The students brought the statue to Tiananmen Square and rallied around it as their symbol of defiance and patriotism.

The student movement received big financial donations from mainland China, Hong Kong, and from overseas Chinese. Many prodemocracy groups outside of China had a strong interest in the students' success. By this stage, the students needed funds to feed and care for more than two hundred thousand people living in squalid conditions on the square. They slept in dirty blankets, one student crammed next to the other. There was very little stepping area. They had only a makeshift bathroom and bathing facilities, and their food delivery and

Leader of the former Soviet Union Mikhail Gorbachev, far right, *arrived in the midst of the huge protest at Tiananmen Square. He met with Deng,* far left, *after having to move past the demonstrators in the square.*

garbage removal was a constant problem. The students tried to organize themselves into work teams, but this was not easy. Different student groups had different goals, and no one understood much about negotiating with an established government.

As the days passed, students were also advised by many older democracy supporters and intellectuals within and outside of China. Several student leaders squabbled about political strategies, and order tumbled into chaos. Some youths came and went from the square, some fought for fame and overreacted in frenzied moments, some became spies for the government, and some even stole funds meant to support participants in the movement.

Inside the government, there was no consensus on what political actions to take. Communist Party secretary general Zhao Ziyang—the most reform-minded high official at the time—was losing power with each day of the demonstration. Deng Xiaoping wanted Zhao to clear away the students efficiently. Zhao, wanting to avoid drastic measures, asked Deng to approve his resignation. Disappointed by his colleague's inaction, Deng would not even talk to Zhao. Zhao went into Tiananmen Square and tearfully told the students that he had come too late, but their problems would be resolved. His

Zhao Ziyang tried to bring the Tiananmen protest to a peaceful end.

statement was not clear, but his regret about imminent government action was obvious.

Deng Xiaoping met with commanders of the Chinese navy and air force. After he secured support for a military crackdown, he ordered premier Li Peng to face the public. On May 20, Li Peng announced martial law—military law used to gain public order in emergencies—in the city.

Martial law meant that demonstrations, strikes, and boycotts were prohibited. Networking and public speaking could be stopped by armed soldiers. Zhao realized he had lost his chance to work peacefully with the students. He knew Deng Xiaoping was in control, and Zhao indicated so publicly. Zhao told people that Deng was the strong arm of the government and was responsible for the military actions.

On May 30, some students voted to call off the demonstrations and clear the square. However, student leaders Li Lu and Chai Ling did not agree to this resolution. Chai Ling felt that by leaving, the students would have gained nothing. As the days passed, she changed her mind often on several issues and called in foreign journalists to publicize her opinions. She and the other leaders no longer had control of the students. In addition, new students were arriving from every part of China, and they did not want the demonstration to end.

By Friday, June 2, three hundred thousand military troops had surrounded Beijing and Tiananmen Square. Citizens began barricading the streets with trash cans, bicycle carts, and anything else they could find. Some people pushed and attacked the soldiers. Others pleaded with stern, silent soldiers not to use guns against their own people. But early on Sunday morning, June 4, the soldiers began firing on demonstrators in Tiananmen Square and the surrounding streets. Tanks rolled into the square, flattening anything or anyone in the way. The soldiers' orders were to clear Tiananmen Square by morning. Killing demonstrators was the method they used.

Gunfire and panic filled the streets surrounding Tiananmen Square. Hours and hours of violence and rage followed throughout the early morning hours of June 4. Hundreds, if not thousands, of people died. The number of dead has never been accurately verified. Journalists caught most of the

Protesting students slept, ate, and discussed their goals in cramped spaces on the square. More protesters joined the demonstration each day.

violence on film, and the world followed China's tragedy on television, radio, and in newspapers.

The tanks did not stop rolling until the streets and the square were emptied. Student leaders went into hiding, and the government immediately began to hunt them down. By July 17, more than forty-six hundred people had been arrested. Twenty-nine of them were executed swiftly.

The protesters at Tiananmen Square hoped to bring democracy to their country, but they discovered that the Communist government would not allow it.

Deng ordered army tanks to roll into Tiananmen Square on June 4, 1989, ending more than one month of prodemocracy protests. Hundreds, perhaps thousands, of citizens were killed, a scene that shocked viewers all over the world.

Deng Xiaoping stayed out of sight during the Tiananmen Square tragedy. Rumors spread that he had fled the city, but these were incorrect. Documents about the event show that Deng was indeed in residence at the end of May and into June. How Deng would be judged by the world after June 4 was an important question.

In a televised speech to the public on June 9, 1989, Deng spoke about the Chinese Communist government's actions at Tiananmen Square. He commended the army and asked Chinese viewers to remember the soldiers—not the students—who were killed.

NINE

SEVENTY PERCENT POSITIVE?

Deng Xiaoping declared that he was not afraid of international criticism of his military crackdown. The June 4 incident, as the 1989 Tiananmen Square violence is called in China, brought severe international reactions. The global media—television, radio, and print—repeatedly recounted the violent events. People on at least six continents could describe China's atrocities. Foreign countries cut off financial aid to China and imposed economic and military sanctions. Many foreign companies canceled business with China.

Despite national and international outrage, Deng did not apologize for his use of military force. He believed that the one-party Communist system was the best for China, and he refused to tolerate any movement toward Western-style democracy. As he said to President Bush at the time, how could China prosper if individual dissent turned into national rebellion? Thousands of Chinese citizens disagreed with Deng, but he was not concerned with their political views.

On June 9, 1989—five days after the Tiananmen massacre—Deng gave a televised speech to the military units that had been called to Beijing to enforce martial law. After asking for a moment of silence to remember the soldiers who had been killed by protesters, he commended the military units for a job well done.

In his speech, Deng defended the patriotic actions of the military. He said, "This shows that the People's Army is truly a great wall of iron and steel of the party and state. This shows that no matter how heavy our losses, the army, under the leadership of the party, will always remain the defender of the country, the defender of socialism, and the defender of the public interest. They are the most lovable people. At the same time, we should never forget how cruel our enemies [prodemocracy students and workers] are. We should have not one bit of forgiveness for them."

After condemning the demonstrators, Deng went on to highlight China's booming economic growth and modernization. He also criticized the United States for its imperfect political system and its condemnation of China's human rights policies. Deng Xiaoping believed that China's internal affairs should not be the concern of foreigners.

Deng thought that the three to five years following 1989 would be the most challenging for the Communist Party in China. He and the central government cracked down on prodemocracy activity by jailing democracy leaders and banning their publications. Deng portrayed the worldwide fall of Communism as a fall into chaos, corruption, economic disaster, food shortage, inflation, and unemployment. Only the negative consequences for countries that had recently abolished Communism were highlighted on Chinese television. This picture influenced many Chinese who feared similar problems in China.

In November 1989, at age eighty-five, Deng announced his full retirement. He celebrated his retirement quietly with his family and a bottle of expensive red wine. Dropping his many titles, however, did not mean that Deng was letting go of authority. He continued to influence the government. Deng selected Jiang Zemin, former mayor and party secretary of Shanghai, as his successor because Jiang was experienced and reform-minded. Politicians still sought Deng's opinion, and he regularly reminded the central government to stay on course, believing that a strong economy would prevent political uprisings.

Like Mao, in his old age Deng began to care about his legacy and reputation. He wanted the final analysis of his work to be primarily positive. He made statements and ordered written reports about the successful economic projects

After Deng's official retirement in 1989, he appointed Jiang Zemin, above left, as General Secretary of the Chinese Communist Party. Jiang is shown here with Deng, right, and Li Peng, second from left, then prime minister of China. Jiang continued the economic reforms that Deng had started.

and political policies he had initiated. However, he ignored the unsuccessful or negative aspects of his career. Deng said many times that his work was approximately 30 percent negative and 70 percent positive, and he could live with that legacy.

From 1989 on, Deng Xiaoping kept a more relaxed pace, spending much of his time with his children and grandchildren. He had kept his family life private, not answering journalists' personal questions and not grooming his children for a career in politics. In his retirement, he allowed a bit more personal information to be publicized. He loved to play with his grandchildren and watch national sports on television. He also played bridge frequently. By that point, the Deng family had eighteen members who all gathered daily for dinner. If one family member was late to the table, the rest had to wait. Deng's was the strongest voice in his family, just as in China.

In 1992 Deng Xiaoping went on one more mission for China. He decided to tour central, southern, and eastern China to witness the economic growth in regions where he had first launched new economic reform. Traveling with Deng Rong, his youngest daughter, who was almost always at his side as he aged, Deng turned his trip into a media event.

Hoping he would be quoted in Hong Kong and in business centers in China, Deng made strong statements about China's economic recovery and stabilized government. He believed that China would be strong when all its people shared equal wealth under a firm Communist government.

On his tour, Deng made a statement that spread throughout the world. He declared that "to get rich is glorious." Hardliners were appalled. To them, Deng sounded dangerously anti-Communist. But Deng believed that successful businesses could contribute to China's overall prosperity. Foreign

Deng, center, foreground, *met with leaders of the Central Committee of the Chinese Communist Party in 1992. Deng's daughter and personal assistant, Deng Rong,* right, *accompanied him almost everywhere in the 1990s.*

business and trade brought in taxes, new technology, and employment—which China needed.

The Hong Kong media quickly picked up Deng's words. Soon people in southern China—who watched Hong Kong television—were motivated by Deng. They wanted to throw their energy into business acceleration. The idea of getting rich caught on in the rest of China too.

Of progress, Deng said, "We must not act like women with bound feet. Once we are sure that something should be done, we should dare to experiment and break a new path.... If we don't have the pioneering spirit, if we're afraid to take risks, if we have no energy and drive, we cannot break a new path, a good path, or accomplish anything new."

Deng's 1992 tour was a national success. In June of that year, the *People's Daily* newspaper reported that all parts of

Deng is shown here at a 1994 Chinese New Year celebration with his daughters Deng Nan, left, and Deng Rong, behind Deng.

the country supported Deng's ideas for economic progress. He was hailed as the architect of reform.

At the fourteenth National Party Congress in October 1992, Deng entered the room on the arm of his daughter. He gave no speech, but delegates applauded him heartily. Deng's reputation—which had been tarnished after the Tiananmen Square violence—was restored for the fourth time.

The National Party Congress may have cheered Deng, but not everyone applauded him or credited him with China's economic growth. When *New York Times* reporter Sheryl Wudunn asked Wei Jingsheng about China's reform, Wei did not hesitate to discredit Deng. About the economic boom in China, Wei said, "This wasn't his [Deng's] initiative. He was pushed into the reforms by popular pressure, he was forced into them. As for the economy doing well, that's not the work of one man. That's the work of the entire nation. So it's not fair to credit Deng Xiaoping personally."

On Thursday, February 20, 1997, the *New York Times* ran a headline that read, "Deng Xiaoping, Architect of Modern China, Dies at 92." He had died the day before in Beijing from Parkinson's disease and complications from lung infections. His death had been expected. Articles on Deng and on China filled at least eight pages of that issue of the *New York Times*. Deng was credited by American editors for being "a political wizard who put China on the capitalist road."

Deng Xiaoping is a hard man to analyze. He did take political steps toward a better economy, steps that no other Chinese Communist leader had taken. He did bring China into the modern international political arena. But what about his brutal invasion of Tibet and his willingness to gun down protesters in Tiananmen Square?

Was Deng Xiaoping's leadership good for China? Many Chinese answer yes. Yet many prodemocracy and human rights advocates call Deng Xiaoping a vicious murderer.

A consensus on Deng is not possible. He was one Chinese leader who led without having a "Mandate from Heaven." Deng Xiaoping was undoubtedly human.

Sources

p. 13   Fox Butterfield, *New York Times,* January 30, 1979, A9.

p. 15   *Time,* February 12, 1979, 16.

p. 23   Benjamin Yang, *Deng: A Political Biography* (New York & London: M. E. Sharpe, 1998), 28. Reprinted by permission from M. E. Sharpe, Inc., Armonk, NY, 10504.

p. 24   Ibid., 28.

p. 27   Deng Mao Mao, *Deng Xiaoping: My Father. (*New York: BasicBooks, HarperCollins Publishers, 1995), 62.

p. 29   Ibid., 80.

p. 31   Yang, 45.

p. 33   Deng Mao Mao, 108.

p. 51   Ibid., photo inset.

p. 52   Yang, 114.

p. 52   Deng Xiaoping, *The Selected Works of Deng Xiaoping, 1938-1992, Vol. I* (Beijing: Foreign Languages Press, 1992), 164.

p. 55   Tenzin Gyatso, *Freedom in Exile: The Autobiography of the 14th Dalai Lama (*New York: HarperCollins, 1990), 224.

p. 57   Stuart R. Schram, ed., *Quotations from Chairman Mao Tse-tung* (New York: Bantam Books, n.d.), 6–7.

p. 64   Deng Xiaoping, *Vol. I,* 293.

p. 65   Yang, 150.

p. 68   Quoted in Richard Evans, *Deng Xiaoping and the Making of Modern China (*London & New York: Penguin Books, 1995), 177.

p. 74   Yang, 172.

p. 78   Ibid., 178.

p. 82   Ibid., 193.

p. 88   Dr. Justin Rudelson, interview by the author, March 29, 1998.

p. 89   Letter given anonymously to author in Beijing, October 1986.

p. 94   Yang, 235–236.

pp. 94–95   Fang Lizhi, "Chinese Democracy: The View from the Beijing Observatory," in *Bringing Down the Great Wall,* edited by James H. Williams (New York: Alfred A. Knopf, 1991), 38.

p. 95   Ibid., 242.

p. 98   Nicholas Kristof and Sheryl Wudunn, *China Wakes: The Struggle for the Soul of a Rising Power* (New York: Times Books-Random House, 1994), 78.

p. 99   Ibid., 79.

pp. 99–100   Interview by the author with Chinese citizen, January 7, 2000.

p. 100   Wang Dan, interview by Canadian TV, May 10, 1989.

p. 102   Interview with Chai Ling in *Gate of Heavenly Peace,* (Brookline, MA: Long Bow Group, Inc., 1995), film.

p. 112   June 9 Speech to Martial Law Units, Beijing Domestic Television Service, June 27, 1989; FBIS June 27, 8–10, <www.nmis.org/Gate/links/#linx1>. (March 3, 1999.)

p. 115   Deng Xiaoping, *Vol. 3,* 360.

pp. 116–117   Kristof and Wudunn, 109.

p. 117   Patrick E. Tyler, "Deng
Xiaoping, Architect of
Modern China, Dies at 92,"
New York Times, February
20, 1997.

Glossary

capitalism: Capitalism is an economic system characterized by private ownership of property and well-developed financial institutions. Capitalism allows individual initiation, business competition, inheritance, and profit earning.

class struggle: Communist theory endorses the elimination of social classes. In order to achieve a classless society, citizens must go through class struggle. They must identify the evils of the dominant class and root out and destroy the causes of social inequality. Class struggle is the process by which to equalize society.

Communism: A governmental system that encourages the elimination of private property and the equitable distribution of goods to the public. A Communist government maintains central control over banking, business, housing, education, industry, medical care, the military, and regional security forces.

Confucianism: A philosophy originating around 500 B.C. and based on the ideas of the Chinese philosopher Confucius (551–479 B.C.). From the 100s B.C. to the A.D. 1900s, Confucianism was the most important single force in Chinese life. It influenced Chinese education, government, personal behavior, and a person's duty to society. Confucius taught that moral behavior was connected to traditional social roles and hierarchies. Each person had set responsibilities to others—ruler and ruled, teacher and student, parent and child, man and woman. Meeting these responsibilities, he believed, would create a virtuous society. Even the highest ruler had obligations to his people. In China, the ruler held the "Mandate from Heaven." This meant that if he did not rule well, the heavens would remove the mandate by striking him down through rebellious citizen action. Confucius taught these ideas to students who came to him for advice, and his students taught their students, so the traditions were passed down. Confucius recorded many of his rules in sayings that were recorded by his students in a short text called *The Analects,* which became the base for Chinese social and political order. Later, *The Analects* were studied and memorized by generations of students. Before the modernization of China's educational system in the early twentieth century, literacy was measured by a person's knowledge and understanding of Confucian texts.

Cultural Revolution: The social upheaval that began in 1966 as a struggle between Mao Zedong and other high-ranking Communist leaders. The movement spread throughout China, and violence frequently broke out as competing radical groups struggled for power. Mao's attempt to put China back on a revolutionary path wrecked the government and economy.

Great Leap Forward: Mao Zedong's dramatic mass organization (1958–1961) to increase industrialization and productivity in China. This movement, based on Mao's belief that human willpower and effort could overcome all obstacles, resulted in economic disaster and widespread starvation.

Guomindang: After the fall of the last empire in China, a new revolutionary government was established in 1912. However, that government was unstable and ever-shifting. The authority was then reorganized into a national political force called the National People's Party, or the Guomindang (sometimes written as Kuomingtang). Members hoped to create a true democratic republic in China. The Guomindang defeated all other political parties in national elections of February 1913. Despite its strength in 1913, the Guomindang's leadership and membership were not stable either. Sun Yatsen reorganized the party, and his death in 1925 led to new leadership by his successor, Chiang Kaishek.

Marxism: Marxism is a political and economic theory of German thinker Karl Marx, who died in 1883. The theory promotes a classless society, the elimination of private ownership, and the provision of work, lodging, and food for all citizens.

Prominent People/Pronunciation Guide

In order to write Chinese names in the Roman alphabet, scholars and diplomats use the pinyin system. This system has been adopted by the United Nations and other international organizations. The pinyin system is pronounced as it looks except that the letter *c* sounds like *ts* and the letter *q* sounds like *ch*. In some cases, an apostrophe is used to distinguish a break in the pronunciation. The pinyin system is used in this book except in cases where names in an older romanization system are more well known. Hyphens in many personal names have also been removed, according to the pinyin system.

Ah Jin	[ah jihn]	Deng's second wife
Chai Ling	[chy ling]	Student leader in 1989
Chiang Kaishek	[jee-ang ky-shehk]	Leader of the Nationalist Party
Deng Danshi	[duhng dahn-shir]	Deng Xiaoping's mother
Deng Lin	[duhng lihn]	Deng's oldest daughter
Deng Nan	[duhng nahn]	Deng's second daughter
Deng Pufang	[duhng poo-fahng]	Deng's first son
Deng Rong	[duhng rohng]	Deng's youngest daughter
Deng Shaosheng	[duhng show-shuhng]	Deng's uncle
Deng Shuping	[duhng shoo-pihng]	Deng's younger brother

121

Deng Wenming	[duhng wehn-mihng]	Deng's father
Deng Xiaoping	[duhng shee-yow-pihng]	Former premier of China
Deng Zhifang	[duhng jee-fahng]	Deng's second son
Fang Lizhi	[fahng lee-jihr]	Prodemocracy Chinese astrophysicist
Hua Guofeng	[hwah gwoh- fahng]	Former premier of China
Huang Hua	[hwoo-ahng hoo-ah]	Foreign Minister in 1979
Hu Yaobang	[hoo yow-bahng]	Former Secretary General of the Chinese Communist Party
Jiang Qing	[jee-ahng ching]	Third wife of Mao Zedong
Jiang Zemin	[jee-ahng dzay-meen]	Deng Xiaoping's political successor
Li Lu	[lee loo]	Student leader in 1989
Lin Biao	[lihn bee-yow]	Military leader, early supporter of Mao
Li Peng	[lee puhng]	Political hard-liner in 1989
Liu Bocheng	[lee-oh boh-chuhng]	Military officer, 129th Division Army

Liu Shaoqi	[lee-oh show-chee]	Communist Party organizer and leader
Mao Zedong	[mow dzay-dohng]	Former Chairman of People's Republic of China
Pu Yi	[poo yee]	Last Manchu emperor of China
Shen Tong	[shuhn tohng]	Student leader in 1989
Sun Yatsen	[soon yaht-sehn]	Leader of China's republican revolution
Wang Chaohua	[wahng chow-hoo-ah]	Student leader in 1989
Wang Dan	[wahng dahn]	Student leader in 1989
Wei Jingsheng	[way jing-shuhng]	Prodemocracy worker and leader of the Democracy Wall movement
Wu-er Kaixi	[woo-ehr ky-shee]	Student leader in 1989
Zhang Xiyuan	[jahng shee-yoo-wehn]	Deng's first wife
Zhao Ziyang	[jow dzih-yang]	Protégé of Deng in 1989
Zhou Enlai	[joh ehn-ly]	Former premier of China
Zhou Lin	[joh lihn]	Deng's third wife

Selected Bibliography

Deng Mao Mao. *Deng Xiaoping: My Father.* New York: BasicBooks, HarperCollins Publishers, 1995.

Deng Xiaoping. *The Selected Works of Deng Xiaoping, 1938–1992, Vols. 1–3.* Beijing: Foreign Languages Press, 1992.

Ebrey, Patricia Buckley. *The Cambridge Illustrated History of China.* Cambridge, England: Cambridge University Press, 1996.

Evans, Richard. *Deng Xiaoping and the Making of Modern China.* London & New York: Penguin Books, 1995.

Fang Lizhi. "Chinese Democracy: The View from the Beijing Observatory." In *Bringing Down the Great Wall.* Edited by James H. Williams. New York: Alfred A. Knopf, 1991.

Goodman, David S. G. *Deng Xiaoping and the Chinese Revolution.* London & New York: Routledge, 1994.

Hsu, Immanuel C. Y. *The Rise of Modern China.* London: Oxford University Press, 1970.

Kristof, Nicholas, and Sheryl Wudunn. *China Wakes: The Struggle for the Soul of a Rising Power.* New York: Times Books-Random House, 1994.

Li Zhisui, with Anne F. Thurston. *The Private Life of Chairman Mao.* New York: Random House, 1994.

Salisbury, Harrison E. *The New Emperors: China in the Era of Mao and Deng.* New York: Avon Books, 1992.

Schell, Orville. *Mandate of Heaven: The Legacy of Tiananmen Square and the Next Generation of China's Leaders.* New York: Simon & Schuster, 1994.

Schram, Stuart R., ed. *Chairman Mao Talks to the People: 1956–1971.* New York: Random House, 1974.

Shambaugh, David, ed. *Deng Xiaoping: Portrait of a Chinese Statesman.* Oxford: Clarendon Press, 1995.

Spence, Jonathan D. *The Search for Modern China.* New York & London: W. W. Norton & Company, 1990.

Tenzin Gyatso. *Freedom in Exile: The Autobiography of the 14th Dalai Lama.* New York: HarperCollins, 1990.

Wei Jingsheng. *The Courage to Stand Alone: Letters from Prison and Other Writings.* New York: Viking, 1997.

Wu, Harry, and Carolyn Wakeman. *Bitter Winds: A Memoir of My Years in China's Gulag.* New York: John Wiley & Sons, Inc., 1994.

Yang, Benjamin. *Deng: A Political Biography.* New York & London: M. E. Sharpe, 1998.

Index

125

Photo Acknowledgments

© New China Pictures/ChinaStock, pp. 2, 90, 92, 97, 113, 115, 116; © Todd Gipstein/CORBIS, p. 6; © Archive Photos, p. 8; © The Bettmann Archive/CORBIS, p. 9; © AP/Wide World Photos, pp. 12, 22, 31, 49, 51, 62, 65, 71, 80, 86, 104, 107; © Dennis Cox/ChinaStock, p. 16; © ChinaStock Photo Library, pp. 19, 36, 54, 60, 83; © CORBIS/Bettmann, pp. 32, 61, 89; © Library of Congress, p. 37; © CORBIS/Bettmann-UPI, pp. 38, 68, 70, 76, 84; © Wu Yinxian/ChinaStock, p. 44; © National Archives, p. 46; © CORBIS Images, pp. 50, 88; © Lu Houmin/ChinaStock, p. 58; © Reuters/CORBIS, p. 73; © Peter Turnley/CORBIS, pp. 101, 108, 109; © Reuters/Herbert Knosowski/Archive Photos, p. 105; © Reuters/Stringer/Archive Photos, p. 110.

Front cover courtesy of © CORBIS/Bettmann-UPI.

About the Author

Always an eager traveler, Whitney Stewart journeys frequently to Asia. In 1986 she and her mother biked all over China and mastered eating with chopsticks. Seeing the Forbidden City in Beijing inspired her to study China's history. Stewart has also met and written about the 14th Dalai Lama of Tibet, Aung San Suu Kyi of Burma, and Sir Edmund Hillary, New Zealand mountaineer.

Acknowledgments:
Several scholars, writers, editors, journalists, and librarians gave their time to answer questions about China: Luke Kwong cheered me and provided answers and source materials; Raymond Lum frequently defined points or looked up texts; anthropologist Justin Rudelson let me audit his course on China at Tulane University and read the finished manuscript for accuracy; Simon Li and several anonymous Chinese students gave me interviews; Ethan Casey, Mary Kay Magistad, and Lobsang Yeshi—all excellent journalists—answered questions and gave me contacts. Chinese author Maggie Huang cheerfully translated Chinese texts on Deng Xiaoping into English. And my editor, Mary Winget, saved me with questions and pointers of her own.

Friends and family members were always supportive: Christiane and Liselotte Andersson offered endless time. Carlin and George Scherer, Richard Stewart and Gwen Washburn, and Cynthia and John Everets listened to my lectures on the perils of biographical writing. Shirley Unwin took me to Tibet and argued about China's history. Writers Lolo Houbein, Marty Ross, Eric Bookhardt, and Sally Rippin kept up inspiring e-mail dialogues. Wangchoi Leung lent me books. Chelle Rudelson browbeat me. The Mayer family always smiled. Cindy Dike of the Maple Street Children's Bookshop told me not to quit. And finally, Hans and Christoph Andersson lived with me patiently as I wrote.

W.S.